If America continues to flirt more with Marx than Moody, we are guaranteed a dystopia of division, along with moral, spiritual, and economic collapse. And Christians will be the most persecuted. The good news is that Drs. Lutzer and Quiggle brilliantly expose the deceptions of Marxism and then reveal the decision we each must make right now . . . before it's too late. This could be the most important book you'll read this year!

Frank Turek
Author and speaker

Marx and Moody offers a powerful reflection on two lives, two legacies, and ultimately, two very different paths for humanity. In a world searching for answers to injustice and inequality, this book thoughtfully examines the consequences of where we place our trust—whether in human systems or in eternal truth. Lutzer and Quiggle challenge readers not only to understand history, but to consider their own role in shaping the future. It is a timely and necessary read.

Kimberly Fletcher
Founder and President, Moms for America

Erwin Lutzer and Gregg Quiggle explain the differences clearly: D. L. Moody saved lives, and Karl Marx disposed of them. D. L. Moody sang that Jesus could have called "ten thousand angels," while Karl Marx was inhabited by ten thousand devils. If you own private property—like this book—you are a follower of Moody, not Marx.

Dave Arnott
Dean of Turning Point USA's Prep Year and host of *The Christian Economist*

The Garden of Eden illustrates a fundamental human choice: to worship God or to worship the handiwork of man. Every individual, in every era, makes this decision, inevitably swayed by the most authoritative voices of their time. In the nineteenth century, contemporaries Karl Marx and Dwight Moody gave this ancient choice a modern expression. By juxtaposing their compelling yet competing messages, Erwin Lutzer and Gregg Quiggle remind readers that the choice remains ever ancient and ever new.

David Weeks
Fletcher Jones Professor of Citizenship and Civic Virtue; Honors College at Azusa Pacific University

There's a growing stack of books in my office calling for attention, and most go unanswered for lack of time. I'm grateful I heeded the call of *Marx and Moody*. This is a book I didn't just read; I devoured it. It sharpened my understanding of two pivotal figures and reminded me that the conflict between good and evil is not abstract; it unfolds on the world stage. Educational. Encouraging. Engrossing. Take the time to read this book.

Todd Friel
Executive Director, Fortis Institute; host of Wretched TV and Radio; pastor, Alpharetta Bible Church

Erwin Lutzer is a brilliant and courageous leader who has written another powerful masterpiece, *Marx and Moody*: two contemporaries, two gospels, two tombstones: one choice. This is a must-read to understand how in England, it was the gospel of Jesus Christ that held back atheistic communism. Christians sharing the message of hope and caring for the needy out of love thwarted socialist attempts to sow divisiveness, discord, and revolution. It is urgent that believers rediscover their vital role in preserving a biblically based society of freedom for the sake of future generations.

William J. Federer
Bestselling author, nationally known speaker

Dr. Erwin Lutzer has unmasked the demon behind Marxism. In typical Lutzer fashion, he lays out the facts simply and takes his readers through a crash-course on both the history and societal effects of Marxism. Lutzer and Quiggle have thoroughly outlined the stark differences between a life lived for Christ and a life lived without Christ, as well as the downstream effect and legacy each of these opposing worldviews hold. This book is critical to understanding the fundamental freedoms we have as Americans, and how these freedoms grant us the liberty to practice our faith and the proclamation of the gospel of Jesus Christ without offense. Every American, every Bible-believing Christian, ought to sit down with this book and absorb it.

Pastor Jack Hibbs
Senior Pastor of Calvary Chapel Chino Hills

In *Marx and Moody*, Erwin Lutzer and Gregg Quiggle brilliantly compare and contrast the influence and impact that these two men of the nineteenth century still have on our culture today. The question becomes—will America trend toward democratic socialism under the influence of Marx, or evangelistic renewal under the influence of Moody? I pray the latter. If you want to better understand this cultural and spiritual battle, then this is a must-read book!

Gary Hamrick
Senior Pastor, Cornerstone Chapel, Leesburg, VA

My friend Erwin Lutzer's latest coauthored book *Marx and Moody* doesn't merely provide a vital history lesson on two of the giants of the nineteenth century, but also dramatically illustrates the nearly infinite gulf between those two figures and their violently opposed worldviews. Anyone unfamiliar with the glorious life of Dwight L. Moody—or with the diabolical nature of Marxism—must read this book!

Eric Metaxas
NYTimes bestselling author of *REVOLUTION*, and host of *Socrates in the City*

Contrast is the mother of clarity, Os Guinness often says. Lutzer and Quiggle have given us a masterclass in exactly that. By placing Karl Marx and D. L. Moody side by side—two men who inhabited the same world, witnessed the same suffering, and reached diametrically opposite conclusions about its cure—they've produced a book that clarifies our current cultural moment with precision. What makes this book especially valuable is that neither author plays it safe: Lutzer grants Marx the legitimacy of his diagnosis before dismantling his prescription, and Quiggle refuses to lionize Moody, honestly reckoning with his shortcomings while lauding his proclamation of a gospel-centered solution. The result is a work that not only informs but also challenges every reader to choose the kind of legacy they will leave.

Abdu Murray
Speaker, author, and President of Embrace the Truth

Erwin Lutzer and Gregg Quiggle have written a remarkable book for our time. Clear, bold, and courageous, *Marx and Moody* combines the scholar's head and the pastor's heart. The gospel of Marxism led to revolutions in the nineteenth century, mass destruction in the twentieth, and still has a foothold in the critical theories and socialist policies of the twenty-first. But it is no match for the gospel of Jesus Christ. In comparing these men, Lutzer and Quiggle paint a picture of death and life, and as D.L. Moody did for tens of millions, they call the reader to choose life.

Cole Feix
Pastor of Carlton Landing Community Church and President of So We Speak

Why did no one write this before now? Given the historical influence and stature of Karl Marx and D. L. Moody, lived out in their shared times, how is it that no one has connected these dots and drawn these observations? Clearly, I really appreciated this important book, Marx and Moody, by Erwin Lutzer and Gregg Quiggle. As Lutzer points out, Marx and Moody shared life on this planet for forty-six years—and those years changed the world. The great Christian evangelist and the father of communism, sharing their times and shaping the modern world, influencing millions for evil and for good. What a story. This is not only an interesting book, it is important. When you read it, you will know why. I commend it highly.

R. Albert Mohler, Jr.
President, The Southern Baptist Theological Seminary

MARX *AND* MOODY

Two Contemporaries. Two Gospels. Two Tombstones. One Choice.

•

ERWIN W. LUTZER *AND*
GREGG WILLIAM QUIGGLE

MOODY PUBLISHERS
CHICAGO

All emphasis in Scripture has been added.

Portions of chapters 7 and 8 in Part One were adapted from *We Will Not Be Silenced* by Erwin Lutzer (Harvest House, 2020).

Edited by Amanda Cleary Eastep
Cover design: Graham Terry
Interior Design: Puckett Smartt
Cover photos: Karl Marx by John Mayall (public domain), Dwight Lyman Moody 1900 by Paul J. Scheips (Library of Congress photo, public domain).

ISBN: 978-0-8024-4013-6

Originally delivered by fleets of horse-drawn wagons, the affordable paperbacks from D. L. Moody's publishing house resourced the church and served everyday people. Now, after more than 125 years of publishing and ministry, Moody Publishers' mission remains the same—even if our delivery systems have changed a bit. For more information on other books (and resources) created from a biblical perspective, go to www.moodypublishers.com or write to:

Moody Publishers
820 N. LaSalle Boulevard
Chicago, IL 60610

1 3 5 7 9 10 8 6 4 2

Printed in the United States of America

We dedicate this book to all who desire to have a better understanding of two famous men who chose divergent paths and left behind radically different legacies. In the process, we wish to challenge each of us to choose the path we take with wisdom and care. All of us are influencers, either for good or for ill; either shining the light of Christ or content with darkness.

Both of us are grateful for our parents who have left us a wonderful godly legacy that we are anxious to pass along to the next generation. To those who will follow us we say, "Therefore as you received Christ Jesus the Lord, so walk in him, rooted and built up in him and established in the faith, just as you were taught, abounding in thanksgiving. See to it that no one takes you captive by philosophy and empty deceit, according to human tradition, according to the elemental spirits of the world, and not according to Christ" (Colossians 2:6–8).

Remember that the only thing that really matters is what matters forever.

CONTENTS

FOREWORD

from Jerry Pattengale

Ten years ago, as the crowd was leaving the sacred hill where the Moodys are buried, one of our nation's most honored preachers knelt alone before their tombs.

It was surreal because he was also the longtime "voice of Moody," the lanky, witty, Rev. Erwin Lutzer. In a sense, for many, he was the nation's preacher much like Dwight L. Moody over a century earlier, and often from those very grounds.

It was also picturesque. The Connecticut River flows just down yonder, with New York on the western horizon, and the heavily wooded Berkshires running northward in the foreground into Vermont.

He was on one knee, praying—and then giving long study of the epigraphs. In a sense, that's where this book began. After reading the following manuscript, I went back through my photos and revisited that freeze-frame day. The obscure knoll where one of the world's most famous preachers, with only a fifth-grade education, was born and died and where his earthly heart never left.

Indeed, that scene sets the stage for not only this book, but the tension and the promise we find when comparing the tandem roles of Dwight L. Moody and Ira Sankey in the late nineteenth century with that of their contemporaries, Karl Marx and Friedrich Engels.

But first, let's peek a bit longer into that day on Moody's sacred ground. Encompassing the kneeling pastor was the sprawling Victorian campus containing Moody's birthplace—just uphill, a simple house perhaps only two football fields from his grave. On the other side of Lutzer and downhill is Moody's home where he died at age sixty-two. Both buildings were easily visible from our perch on Roundtop on the outskirts of remote Northfield, Massachusetts.

As Rev. Lutzer prayed, also taking in the moment with me was one of the foremost authorities on Moody, Gregg Quiggle. Both he and Lutzer were connected to Moody through respect, lifelong study, and via their long careers at Moody Bible Institute and The Moody Church in Chicago—nearly 1,000 miles away.

I was privileged to sit for long stretches as they reminisced about the lives of the Moodys there in northwest Massachusetts. They would help me reimagine the thousands of people who would converge each summer on the campus that Moody, Sankey, and friends built for disadvantaged girls. And another campus for boys just five miles away.

However, after perusing the many photo albums from the school's apex (around the time of Moody's passing) and listening to several septuagenarians and octogenarians share about the glory days of those summer camps and revivals that lingered on for decades, the stark reality hit anew—that campus had been empty for nearly twenty years. My role was to help find a worthy organization to receive it as a gift, and we were there to celebrate that transition.

That campus's rise and fall, and rise, sets the stage for what you're about to read. First, let me share one more story from that hallowed hill called Roundtop—a place to this day where tour buses stop for admirers, including many from Asian countries. They are often spiritual descendants of Moody's preaching, a journey you'll learn more about over Quiggle's shoulder.

Surrounded by other dignitaries that day was the esteemed and bow-tied Woody White, president of the Cecil B. Day Foundation. After Rev. Lutzer finished his careful study of the tombs, we began a festive transition to tour the stunning campus buildings.

In a lighter moment, I urged White to share his bizarre encounter with a witch on Roundtop just a couple of years earlier. While stopping with a friend to show him their graves, Woody noticed a witch, a story I captured elsewhere. "She jumped up from lying across D. L. Moody's tombstone. Her cape went horizontal, and my friend Woody White about followed suit. Her black-streaked hair and dark curly fingernails enhanced the shock."

She was "grave soaking," or trying to block and/or steal the blessing from Moody. This thirtysomething intruder was dishonoring the legendary evangelist's tomb. When she fled, Woody chased her until she nosedived into fescue during her downhill sprint near "Martyrs' Grove"—planted for the twenty-one women martyrs (on mission fields) associated with the campus.

Somewhere between Moody's passing and the mid-1900s, not only that little borough but much of New England had changed. White was intimately aware, having visited numerous churches in the Northeast for his foundation, and speaking with pastors and lay leaders about congregational life in Northfield and beyond.

Dr. James Spencer, also present that day, is now president of the D. L. Moody Center, housed in Moody's manse. He noted that 56 percent of individuals living in Boston, MA, were classified as *post-Christian* by Barna. Of the 20 cities Barna classified in the *top 10 post-Christian cities in the America*, 14 were within 200 miles of Northfield, MA.

Keep in mind that the Northfield campus is as gorgeous and pronounced as other signature campuses—and yet lost its way, at least its spiritual moorings. The town itself is dominated by Unitarians. Kind, many are friends, but accepting of all paths to heaven.

Eventually, the path to Moody's Northfield campus for revivalists became overgrown. Ironically, he became the progenitor for today's Moody campus four states away. His message long outlived the messenger, but the foundation transcends any brick and mortar.

What is riveting about this new book's comparison is that thousands of people have toured the tomb of Marx in London. Likewise, throngs have knelt on Roundtop and hundreds of thousands have held worship services there. But the lights went on for an inveterate septuagenarian preacher from Chicago as he stood in Marx's tomb, realizing Marx and Moody were contemporaries, and the contrasting legacy of their worldviews.

An insightful few pages ahead are letters from Marx and Engels commenting on their disdain for Spurgeon and Moody—and religious belief in general. Engels even gives a detailed description of why he thinks Moody was winning crowds whereas Marxism failed to take root in the Isles.

Lutzer and Quiggle give an engaging outline of the divergent paths of these two pairs of influencers—the horrific ills of Marxism and Socialism (the revolution), and the personal and institutional effects of Christianity. And in the latter lies the key for Americans.

Institutions are systematic responses to recurring needs, and key targets of Socialists en route to worldwide Communism. Lutzer has outlined in many of his books the positive influences of Christianity—and much of them are linked to the institutions built on its precepts, starting of course with the church. Our textbook for Museum of the Bible (DC) does the same—*The Bible's Influence of Western Civilization* (2026).

When I finished my first reading of this Lutzer-Quiggle gem, I immediately contacted a few key influencers, recommending that copies reach as many pastors and religious leaders as possible. Obviously, the timeliness of this prompts such a suggestion given the head-scratching rise of "Democratic Socialism."

What these authors do well is show step-by-step the false claims of Marxism, the ultimate underpinning of upstart variants in the United States. The revolutionary strategy of ends justifying the means. The absence of any sense of truth. The façade of innocence—ignoring links to horrific evil leaders via contemporary charismatic voices. Likewise, the book's second half grounds us in the person of Moody and anchors his story and the biblical message writ large. Pause and carefully read the book's table of contents, and you'll have a roadmap for what's ahead—and if you're like me, will want to jump ahead to find the authors' insights on today's pressing political questions.

Two sections especially help readers in this reemergence in America of errant political ideologies. In the first half Lutzer outlines succinctly Marxist pillars, or "six useful lies." Again, it's impossible to grasp the evil ends ahead for those promoting offshoots of this in American politics without grasping these half-dozen deceits. 1) Equality surfaces when private property is abolished. Be aware of politicians using "Collective Good" or "Collectivism," as we've learned plenty from Stalin and others how such ends. 2) Transfer belief in God to belief in the State. Yes, mass graves for dissenters abound in socialist countries. 3) Abolish the family. It makes one dizzy just trying wrap your mind around this. 4) Throw out all "historic" truth and let the State create new truth. 5) The mandate for a violent revolution. In essence, the call for "all workers to unite" (whatever that really means) is ipso facto to slaughter dissenters. And, 6) create a borderless world. This concept ignores a key reason most civilizations ceased to exist.

The second half of the book shows us Moody's journey from poverty, like many of the oppressed and desperate workers to whom Marx and Engels were appealing. However, the authors acknowledge the societal ills and greed of a few that indeed exacerbated matters, especially in London. However, Moody introduced them to hope in Christ, not some artificial incoherent ideological construct. He championed the dual appointment of Christians to share both the gospel and their gifts (material and spiritual), though ultimately to address the human journey—"Ruined," "Redeemed," and "Regenerated."

Let me end with recollections of two others among the crowd at Roundtop that day. Emmitt Mitchell is a smiling elder statesman with a long history of financial success. He was also the leader of the National Black Caucus under President Reagan and later helped start the stalwart donor advised fund with Bill High, now called Signatry. Emmitt has given much of the last decade helping to marshal the memory of Moody through that property. He also understands the irony that hundreds of thousands who have visited Northfield, and the millions who have heard Moody preach, changed their communities for good even if the local community lost touch with its spiritual roots, accented in part by the empty campus.

The other person there in all his glory was David Powell III—the ranking direct descendant of D. L. Moody. With each passing year he would bring more and more memorabilia to our Northfield meetings and often commented on how he had to live long enough to appreciate fully the effects of his great-grandfather's teachings. Most of those mentioned above attended David's funeral in 2022. Fittingly, it was close to the Northfield campus, in a church with "Trinity" in its name, and the main song at his request, "Blest Be the Tie That Binds."

—**Jerry Pattengale,** Founding Scholar, Museum of the Bible (DC); first University Professor, Indiana Wesleyan University (f. 1920); and Author

TIMELINE

1818	Karl Marx born in Trier, Germany
1820	Friedrich Engels born in Barmen, Germany
1835	Marx goes to the University of Bonn, Germany
1837	Dwight L. Moody born in Northfield, Massachusetts
1837	Queen Victoria crowned Queen of England
1841	Marx receives a Doctor of Philosophy degree from University of Jena
1843	Marx marries and moves to Paris
1843	Charles Dickens releases *A Christmas Carol*
1848	Marx publishes *The Communist Manifesto* with coauthor Friedrich Engels
1849	Marx moves to London after being banned from Germany, Belgium, and France
1852	*Uncle Tom's Cabin* published
1855	Moody converted in Boston
1856	Moody moves to Chicago
1858	Moody starts Sunday School in Chicago
1859	Darwin publishes *On the Origin of Species*
1860	Abraham Lincoln elected President
1861	Charles Dickens publishes *Great Expectations*
1861–65	US Civil War
1865	Lincoln assassinated
1862	Moody marries Emma Charlotte Revell
1867	Marx publishes *Das Kapital Vol. 1*
1871	Great Chicago Fire

1873–75	Moody and Ira D. Sankey's Great Campaign in the UK and Ireland
1876	Alexander Graham Bell invents the telephone
1879	Thomas Edison invents the electric light
1883	Marx dies in London
1885	*Das Kapital Vol. II* published posthumously (edited by Engels)
1893	Moody at Chicago World's Fair
1892	Tchaikovsky's *The Nutcracker* premiers
1894	*Das Kapital Vol. III* published posthumously (edited by Engels)
1898	Spanish-American War
1899	Moody dies in Northfield
1901	Queen Victoria dies

PART ONE

KARL MARX

DR. ERWIN LUTZER

Introduction from Erwin Lutzer

Karl Marx is one of the most consequential political philosophers in history. Lest anyone think that philosophers sit in ivory towers and write abstract theories, think again. Philosophers have greatly influenced history, and none has done this more radically than Karl Marx.

Marx connected his philosophy with economics and wrote a document intended to rectify systemic economic abuses that were rampant in England and Europe. But unfortunately, when his purposed solution was applied, it resulted in the most barbaric and evil revolutions possible. And tragically, he still rules much of the world from his grave.

Marx was influenced by the philosopher Friedrich Hegel who posited that reality was always in flux, there was a dialectic at work meaning that opposites were always coming together and thus evolving onward and upward in the spiral of history. This meant that truth was never fixed but in transition; something that was true today could be false tomorrow. Marx took that idea of dialectics and applied it to the economic disparities between classes, believing that as they clashed, something better would arise. But this premise was wrong-headed, and as a result, rather than improving the injustices of the world, his philosophy gave birth to even greater evils.

This book you hold in your hands deals only with the seminal document, *The Communist Manifesto*. Various books explaining the breadth of Marx's writings, including the massive three-volume *Das Kapital*, have been ably written by others. But it is *The Manifesto* that crystallizes in a more popular style the essence of the revolution that Marx and his coauthor Friedrich Engels called for.

Comparing Karl Marx and Dwight L. Moody is not just a study of contrasting worldviews, but in a larger sense, it is a cameo of a much larger and fiercer war being fought in the invisible world, a war that began when Lucifer fell out of favor with God and became His eternal antagonist. When we encounter Marx, we know that we are met with not only a failed human philosophy but one empowered by malevolent forces beyond this world. In Moody, we meet a man who cannot be explained except by the unique and life-changing message of the gospel of God. And his legacy has led millions into the enjoyment of eternal life.

So, as you read, remember that there are really only two worldviews: one that sees God as the ultimate reality and the other that puts man at the center of his world. And, given the limitations of human reason and the reality of inborn sin, mankind is bound to manage his failures with various degrees of success. Whenever man substitutes himself for God, the idol he has formed will not only disappoint but will end in destruction.

Jesus contrasted the two basic worldviews: "The thief comes only to steal and kill and destroy. I came that they may have life and have it abundantly" (John 10:10).

Let's learn from the past and make sure we are following the right path.

CHAPTER 1

My Visit to Two Graves

Two Lives, Two Legacies

It has been my privilege to stand at the graves of two influential past contemporaries and contemplate their radically different views regarding the meaning of life, the plight of humanity, and how we should think about right and wrong. The lessons these two men left behind force us to ask similar questions about ourselves, what we should strive for in life, and the legacy we will leave behind.

As the former senior pastor of The Moody Church in Chicago, I have often visited the grave of D. L. Moody in Northfield, Massachusetts, pondering how this man with such a poor and humble background nevertheless influenced millions of people with the simple transforming message of the gospel. On Sundays, I would walk into the beautiful sanctuary of The Moody Church, which was constructed and dedicated twenty-six years after his death, and ask myself how a man with such a limited education could have such a continuing worldwide impact. Many years ago, I also taught at Moody Bible Institute, experiencing the ongoing influence of D. L. Moody though his education initiatives. His work and vision are part of a legacy that still affects lives today.

Later in this book, I will comment on what is engraved on his tombstone and that of his wife, Emma. The snatches of Scripture written there speak volumes of a glorious future for those who serve the Lord. The more I learn about Moody, the more inspired I am to be faithful to the gospel.

More recently, I stood at the grave of Karl Marx in Highgate Cemetery in London, England. It was a chilling reminder that one man in defiance of God can do incalculable damage to entire countries. I'm intrigued by his faith in his political and economic ideology that would eventually form the foundation of communist regimes, oppressing millions over the last century. Marx said he wanted to liberate the people from economic disparities, yet he ended up choking them with a form of totalitarianism that not only led to campaigns like Lenin's Red Terror but prompted the killing of millions of people. Later, I shall also share the words engraved on Marx's tomb. Sadly, his ideas still rule much of the world from beyond the grave.

I was struck by the fact that these two men were contemporaries. Moody was a few years younger than Marx, but they shared life on this planet for forty-six years. No doubt, Marx heard of Moody, who preached in London from 1875 through 1879 and whose ministry and sermons were front-page news. Marx probably never attended one of Moody's meetings because he was spending most of his time in the British Museum Reading Room (now the British Library), writing the first volume of *Das Kapital* (in English, *Capital*), a defense of his economic theory. (The last two volumes were published posthumously, completed by Friedrich Engels, Marx's devotee and coauthor of *The Communist Manifesto*.)

But we know that Engels did attend a Moody meeting.

Engels Attends Moody's Meeting

In a letter to Eduard Bernstein, dated February 11, 1879 (thirty-one years after *The Communist Manifesto* was released), Engels describes his experience in a searing recounting of the event:

> The English working class is apathetic, and the trade unions are doing nothing. The social movement is at a standstill, and the socialist propaganda is making no headway. The only thing that is flourishing is the religious revival, which is sweeping the country like a plague. On Sunday evening I was at Moody and Sankey's—a huge barn of a place (the Agricultural Hall) holding about 20,000 people, packed full. The preacher is a tall, thin American with a strong nasal twang, who speaks very simply and without any theological frills, but practical and often not without wit. The singing is led by a choir of 500 voices, accompanied by a harmonium and a cornet, and the hymns are simple and catchy, with choruses that the whole audience can join in. The audience is mostly lower-middle class and working class, with a sprinkling of the upper crust who come out of curiosity. *The whole thing is a masterpiece of mass psychology, and the emotional effect is tremendous. The people are worked up to a pitch of excitement, and at the end there is an appeal for conversions, and hundreds of people come forward to "give their hearts to Jesus." It is a sight to make one think, and it shows how deep the religious instinct is in the English people. But it also shows how the ruling class uses religion to keep the masses in check. The whole performance is a clever piece of stage management, and the Americans are past masters at it.*[1] (Emphasis added)

Keep those words in mind: "It also shows how the ruling class uses religion to keep the masses in check." As we will discuss, that theme had received a great deal of attention in *The Communist Manifesto*, written years earlier.

Years later, as Engels neared the end of his life, he reminisced as to why the revolution called for in the *Manifesto* had not happened in England. In other words, the proletariat (the working class) had refused the call to revolt against the bourgeoisie (the owners). He accused the bourgeoisie of using religion as a trade by importing men like Moody and Ira Sankey (Moody's music leader) from America, and also accepting "the dangerous aid of the Salvation Army, which revives the propaganda of early Christianity, appeals to the poor as the elect, fights Capitalism in a religious way, and fosters an element of early Christian class antagonism, which one day may become troublesome to the well-to-do people who now find the ready money for it."[2]

In a somewhat begrudging way, Engels admits that the refusal of England to join in a communist revolution could be blamed on Christian ministries, among them the "dangerous aid" of the Salvation Army. Evidently, he believed that by meeting the needs of the poor, the Salvation Army had satisfied the needs of the working class (the proletariat), so they saw no reason to rise up and overthrow the capitalists. Although Engels does not mention it, we should also note that the YMCA was begun in England in 1844, initially as a constant round of Bible studies for young men to keep them from the temptations of the streets. The organization also provided help for the needy. Just over ten years later, a similar organization was begun for women, the YWCA, which empowered them with education and helped with work-related challenges.[3] Christians, such as George Mueller

(1805–1898), built orphanages and schools, and churches stressed the need for individual Christian outreach and compassion. We can confidently say the major reason Britain didn't exchange the Bible for *The Communist Manifesto* was because of the country's deep Christian roots. In other words, there simply were not enough revolutionaries in England willing to kill and pillage as the communist manifesto required to bring about the overthrow of the ruling class.

In addition, the years Marx and Engels were in London were coincident with the ministry of the great nineteenth-century preacher, Charles Spurgeon. That Marx and Engels would have known about Spurgeon's ministry is obvious. For example, Engels participated in a popular Victorian parlor game called Confessions (inspired by Jean-Jacques Rousseau's *Confessions*), in which participants listed likes and dislikes in response to prompts. In response to the prompt "the characters you most dislike" (or "Die Charaktere, die du am meisten verabscheust" in the original German), Engels wrote a single word: "Spurgeon."[4] The German word *verabscheuen* means "to detest, to abhor, to loathe."[5] Marx and Engels almost certainly would have had the same contempt for the famous D. L. Moody as they did for the London preacher.

The Great Contrast

The contrast between Marx/Engels and Moody could not have been greater, and the lessons they left behind are as divergent as night and day. Marx was only able to destroy; he was not able to build a better life for the people he sought to help. Moody preached a message of liberation from sin that set people free; he preached Christ as the One who could give them eternal life and lead them to an eternity with God. Marx was highly educated; Moody had, at best, a fifth-grade education and had to work hard improving his reading as time went by.

These two men represent two opposing worldviews that have competed in the annals of history and will continue to clash in the final showdown as the future winds down. For those of us who believe the Scriptures, the outcome is not in doubt.

The "ghost" of Karl Marx cannot be ignored here in America. We will find the infiltration of Marxist ideas even in unlikely places. In the pages to follow, we will discover the seduction of Marxism not just in the political world but also in our schools, and yes, even in our churches.

So, what did Marx teach and what did his friend Friedrich Engels believe was his mentor's enduring legacy? Let's go to the cemetery and find out.

The Eulogy: High Praise for the Man in the Grave

On Saturday, March 17, 1883, his faithful followers gathered for a funeral service for Karl Marx in Highgate Cemetery in London. Standing there with a few people around him was Friedrich Engels who gave this glowing assessment of his beloved friend and mentor. Let's listen in:

> On the 14th of March, at a quarter to three in the afternoon, the greatest living thinker ceased to think. He had been left alone for scarcely two minutes, and when we came back we found him in his armchair, peacefully gone to sleep—but for ever.[6]

Engels said that Marx's death was "an immeasurable loss" and "this mighty spirit will soon enough make itself felt."[7] He went on to say that Marx was attempting to rectify abuses, to find a solution to the exploitation of the working class by the bourgeoisie (the land and factory owners), and his solution would be implemented worldwide. The elite bourgeoisie was inflicting injustice on the abused workers called the proletariat. The Industrial Revolution had exacerbated the gap between the haves and the have-nots; between the rich owners and the workers paid starvation wages. Something had to be done. Engels continued,

> Marx was before all else a revolutionary. His real mission in life was to contribute, in one way or another, to the overthrow of capitalist society and of the state institutions which it had brought into being, to contribute to the liberation of the modern proletariat, which he was the first to make conscious of its own position and its needs.[8]

But Marx had critics. Engels said these "he brushed aside as though it were cobweb, ignoring it, answering only when extreme necessity compelled him. And he died beloved, revered and mourned by millions of revolutionary fellow-workers—from the mines of Siberia to California, in all parts of Europe and America. . . . His name will endure through the ages, and with it his work!"[9]

At the 100th anniversary of Marx's death, Philip Foner (1910–1994), an American Marxist known for his aggressive support of Marxism and the labor movement, spoke of the positive impact of Marxism. In his preface to a collection of responses to the anniversary, Foner praised Marx's writings as "the most influential body of thought in the world. Hundreds of millions live in societies whose fundamental principles—Socialism—were laid down over a century ago by Karl

Marx and his collaborator and friend, Friedrich Engels."[10] He added, "I am confident that when the 200th anniversary of the death of Karl Marx will be observed, the entire world will be Socialist."[11]

With accolades like that, we must consider: What exactly was Marx's philosophy? No matter what we might say about him, his impact on society has been, and still is, massive. Everywhere you go, there are discussions of Marxism and how it should be applied to an economy and our cultural norms. And more ominously, his philosophy has contributed to the political views of regimes in charge of millions of people in countries around the world. Today, with Democratic Socialism in the news, we had better understand its Marxist roots.

So, what was this man's philosophy? Why did he believe the lies he so confidently espoused? Why did his philosophy appear to be an answer to legitimate societal problems? And what is their continuing impact?

Why This Book?

This book is a joint project. Dr. Gregg Quiggle, PhD, a former professor at Moody Bible Institute, is an expert on D. L. Moody and has written a book about him. As a historian, Gregg is able to put Moody into his cultural and social context, describing his unlikely background and the incredible breadth and impact of his ministry. He has written the section on Moody.

I have written the section on Karl Marx, having had an interest in him and his ideas ever since I was required to read *The Communist Manifesto* while a philosophy major at university. I have just recently reread it carefully with new eyes and a new understanding. And, as such, I see more clearly the seduction of Marxism and how its influence is still being felt.

Both Marx and Moody lived during a time of industrialization and urbanization, when people were moving into the cities, and factories were being built with markets for their goods increasing worldwide. Workers were being exploited, wages were low, and yet the hours of work per week increased. Poverty was everywhere.

Marx thought he had a solution to this exploitation; he believed it was possible for everyone to share equally in an increasingly prosperous world. As we will discover, there are reasons why his solution became a curse to the world.

Moody did not ignore these realities. Unlike Marx, he was brought up in poverty and knew firsthand the debilitating effects of growing up without proper food and clothes, and with only a fifth-grade education. As we shall see, he was both directly and indirectly involved in social action, but with different values and an eternal perspective. Moody did not just care about people's souls; he also cared about their living conditions.

What do we intend to accomplish in the pages ahead? Put simply, this book showcases the difference between a man-centered worldview and a God-centered worldview. In the process, we will critique Marxism through the lens of the Bible regarding God, human nature, and His solution for the evils of society, then compare Marx's message with that of Moody. Second, we want people to understand that politics matters—good government cannot save us, but bad government can hinder, if not destroy, the witness of the church. Third, we will see that ideas have consequences and we will consider what

Marx got wrong and Moody got right.

Finally, and most importantly, we shall explain what is written on the tombstones of these two men and ask ourselves: What do I want written on *my* tombstone? What will *my* legacy be? *And, a hundred years from now, what will I wish I had done today?*

In this first section of this book, let us take the time to explore the teaching of one of the most influential philosophers in history. Let us uncover the ideas that made him a household name, both loved and hated. We are influenced by him in ways we do not even know about, and in ways we might not understand. He is a man we dare not ignore.

Keep reading.

CHAPTER 2

A Father and Mother's Concern for Their Son

Is Your Demon Heavenly or Faustian?

There was a question Karl Marx's father, Heinrich, asked his son Karl when he was eighteen years old. In a moment we will read the context of the question and ponder its implications. But first, a bit of Marx's early history.

Karl Marx was born in 1818 to Jewish parents in the town of Trier in the Rhineland of Germany. The town was 90 percent Catholic; his father converted from Judaism to the Lutheran faith, possibly to avoid Jewish persecution. And it is speculated that he chose Lutheranism over Catholicism because this would give him more latitude of thought. Be that as it may, their young son Karl was baptized Lutheran at the age of five or six.

Marx attended a religious preparatory school for a time and was considering the Lutheran ministry. He is quoted as saying, "Our heart, reason, intelligence history all summon us with loud and convincing voice to the knowledge that union with Him [Christ] is absolutely necessary, that without Him we would be unable to fulfill our purpose, that without Him we would be rejected by God, and only He can redeem us."[1]

That is high praise for Christ.

But as many parents have learned, children can turn away from their upbringing, especially when they come in contact with radical ideas promoted in universities by those who remain safely exempt from the consequences of their ideas. There, enticed by ideas that sound good to the natural mind and throwing off the supposed restraints of Christianity, a young adult may soon abandon whatever faith they may have. So, as Marx was introduced to radicals on his intellectual journey, he found reasons to question his religious training and "deconstructed" (to use a contemporary term). He would come to hate God and end up advocating for atheism, imposing his theories through forced conformity.

Young Karl, growing up in a Lutheran home and attending the Lutheran church in Trier, would have been well acquainted with Martin Luther. After all, he would have been taught German history, and who can overlook the massive impact of Luther in Germany? Luther's work represented a turning point, a milestone in Germany's history. The minority Lutherans in Trier would have had high regard for Luther's writings; even which church they attended was the result of his continuing impact.

In 1844, when Marx was just twenty-six, he wrote *Zur Kritik der Hegelschen Rechts-Philosophie* (*A Contribution to the Critique of Hegel's Philosophy of Right*). In it, Marx wrote about Martin Luther, believing he had begun the first phase of a revolution: Luther had overcome the bondage of religious devotion to the church, now Marx would free the people from the economic bondage of Capitalism. Luther had freed people within their hearts, what remained was the need for a revolution that would free the people from the economic servitude imposed by the bourgeoisie who owned the means of production such as the land and the factories.

In Marx's mind, if a monk could start a revolution, he, a philosopher, could as well. But the revolution Marx began would be radically different from that of Martin Luther. Yes, *radically* different.

But I'm ahead of the story . . .

The Foreboding of a Concerned Father

Let's pause for a deep breath and return our attention to Karl Marx when he was still in his teens, before he left home to become a radical. Karl Marx's father, Heinrich, felt a sense of foreboding when he thought about his teenage son. When Karl was eighteen, he received a letter from his father:

> At times I cannot rid myself of ideas which arouse in me sad forebodings and fear when I am struck as if by lightning by the thought: is your heart in accord with your head, your talents? Has it room for earthly but gentler sentiments . . . And since that heart is obviously *animated and governed by a demon not granted to all men, is that demon heavenly or Faustian*? . . . will you ever be capable of truly human, domestic happiness? Will—and this doubt has no less tortured me recently since I have come to love a certain person like my own child—will you ever be capable of imparting happiness to those immediately around you?[2] (Emphasis added).

That "certain person" mentioned in the last sentence is Jenny, whom Marx was dating and would later marry. Evidently his father saw something troubling within his eighteen-year-old son. Little did his father realize that Karl would not only create unhappiness with those around him, but misery for millions. His philosophy, given life under Lenin and Stalin, would bring starvation, death, and torture to Russia and numerous other countries, even to this day.

"Is that demon heavenly or Faustian?"

What comes to mind at the mention of the name Faust? Quite probably you think of the sixteenth-century legend of the man who made a pact with the devil, traded his soul for earthly knowledge rather than divine knowledge, and lost his soul to hell. If that came to your mind, you would be correct, but that is not the Faust the Marx family were reading about in their home. This story of Faust came two hundred years later, written by a famous man of the German Enlightenment, Johann Wolfgang von Goethe, was one of the most influential writers in Germany and of the German Enlightenment.

As I write, my mind goes back years to the time when I had the privilege of visiting the house of Goethe in Weimar, Germany. As you walk into the house, which is now a museum, you are met by a series of gradually more expansive doorways until, at the end of the large room, you see a statue of a man, a colossus signifying the exaltation of mankind and a man no longer subject to the church or bound by cultural morals, but rather a man who is free—very free. A man who is, in effect, "the master of his fate / the captain of his soul."[3]

There we learned how Goethe reworked the original story of *Faust*, giving his version an ending more consistent with the Enlightenment. Goethe revised this play a few times, so some of the details vary, but the bottom line is that Faust makes a pact with the devil (Mephistopheles), agreeing to give the devil his soul in exchange for an endless array of pleasures. The devil insists that Faust sign the pact with his own blood. Despite Faust's initial resistance, he does finally agree to do so. So as promised, in the quest for pleasure, Mephistopheles helps Faust meet an innocent young lady named Gretchen, then guides Faust in seducing her step by step. Eventually, Gretchen becomes pregnant; when the baby is born, Gretchen, overcome with guilt, kills the child. Rather than face death at the hands of the executioners for having committed murder, she commits suicide.

There are other details, but here is the point: In the end, an angel intervenes and thereby Faust outwits the devil, and Faust is welcomed into heaven because, of all things, Gretchen is praying for him in heaven. He is saved by the prayers of the woman whom he had seduced and deceived!

Don't miss the point of this version of *Faust*: *You can sell your soul to the devil in exchange for all the pleasures of the world and still win in the end!*

As we shall see, throughout the early writings of Marx, he frequently wrote about themes such as pacts with the devil, suicide, and defiance of God. As you read, keep in mind a line in *Faust*, frequently quoted by Marx: "All that has come into existence deserves to be destroyed."[4] Please notice it does not say, "All that has been *created* deserves to be destroyed"; that would imply a Creator. But simply that everything that has "come into existence."

More about that later.

After Marx left home to attend the University of Bonn (then, the University of Berlin), it appeared to his parents that Faustian demons were plaguing young Karl and were increasingly agitating him. In 1837, he wrote his father a long letter and said, "When I left you, a new world had begun to exist for me, that of love, which in the beginning was intoxicated with longing and devoid of hope."[5] Near the end of the letter he writes that that the candle at his table had gone out and he could no longer read what he had written; he concluded, "A deep unrest has mastered me and I shall not be able to lay [down] the specters that haunt me until I am in your dear presence."[6]

Not that Karl had a great deal of respect for his father; indeed, even in his letter he was dismissive and exhibited contempt for the old man. A few weeks later, his father wrote back, excoriating his son for his lack of respect and the mess his son was making of his life. That letter begins,

> God's grief!!! Disorderliness, musty excursions into all departments of knowledge, musty brooding under a gloomy oil-lamp; running wild in a scholar's dressing-gown and with unkempt hair . . . running wild over a glass of beer; unsociable withdrawal with neglect of all decorum and even of all consideration for the father. . . . *I must and will say that you have caused your parents much vexation and little or no joy . . . you spend your nights giving birth to monsters.*[7] (Emphasis added).

Karl's father was angry that his son had been squandering money and always came begging for more. Heinrich berates him for being thankless; for disregarding any attention to his brothers and sisters, and yet, he ended by saying that if Karl came home, he would be welcomed with "open arms." With that, the letter closes.

His father died a few months later at the age of fifty-six.

Karl, living in Berlin at the time, did not attend his father's funeral. Some believe it was out of spite.

His father saw what others might not have seen: His son Karl was "giving birth to monsters."

The Consternation of His Mother

"[I wish that] Karl would accumulate capital [money] instead of just writing about it."[8] Those are the words of an exasperated mother who was tired of her son constantly begging her for money. With his father dead, Karl turned to his mother, Henrietta, repeatedly, pressuring her for funds, and as his demands for money continued, his mother expressed frustration with her wayward son. When he did make his first visit to his mother in twenty years, it was for money. He wrote to his wife, "She does not want to hear a word about money but she destroyed the I.O.U.'s that I made out to her; that is the only pleasant result of the two days I spent with her."[9]

While she forgave Karl's promises to repay previous loans, she evidently did not give him more money. He had once told her that if she didn't intervene to cover his many debts with the landlady, shopkeepers, and the pub, that he would return to Prussia (a predominate state in Germany in which Marx was born and the family lived) and let the police arrest him; but Henrietta did not budge.[10] But all was not lost for Karl. With the help of a lawyer, he received a generous sum of the money she left when she died in March of 1853.

Don't miss this: Five years earlier in 1848, when *The Communist Manifesto* was released, it insisted on the "abolition of all right of inheritance."[11] In other words, Marx thought it was unfair for a child to inherit wealth from his parents because that would breed inequality; after all, everyone should start out in life "equal." Yet, Marx insisted that he get his mother's wealth. This is an example of "Rules for thee, but not for me" that we see among all egomaniacs throughout history.

With the death of his parents, Marx now turned to other sources of income, primarily from his wealthy friend and disciple, Frederich Engels, whom he had met in Paris. Marx was continually begging him for money. Through all of this, we can see that Marx envied those with wealth.

Marx and His Family

So, how well did Marx take care of his own family? Simply put, they suffered because Karl didn't have a job, though he did earn some living from writing articles and editing a paper. But his wife and children lacked food, decent clothes, and basic necessities. They survived only because of friends who helped them financially. Because their conditions were deplorable, it's no wonder Marx wrote to Engels, "Every day my wife says she wishes she and the children were in their graves, and I really cannot blame her, for the humiliations, torments and alarums that one has to go through in such a situation are indeed indescribable."[12]

A year after the publication of *The Communist Manifesto*, Marx's landlord evicted him for not paying the rent. Historian Paul Kengor writes that "the landlord was also fed up with Marx's resistance to grooming. Karl drank too much, smoked too much, never exercised, and suffered from warts and boils from his lack of washing. He stunk."[13] Then quoting a Prussian police spy, Kengor continues, "Washing, grooming and changing his linens are things he does rarely, and he likes to get drunk . . . everything is broken down . . . in a word, everything is topsy-turvy."[14]

His wife, Jenny, herself agreed with her husband's contempt for religion (if not his hygiene). They did not pass on any religious faith to their six children and instead indoctrinated them in radical political philosophy. Most of their six children suffered tragic ends, and only two daughters survived their father.

Their daughter Elenor poisoned herself after learning of her husband Edward Aveling's infidelity. He convinced her to enter a suicide pact with him and die in one another's arms. Elenor followed through with the plan and died on March 31, 1898, but Edward did not. With his wife dead, he inherited all the wealth that Elenor had been bequeathed by her father, including book royalties and valuable papers.[15]

Thirteen years later, on November 25, 1911, his daughter Laura died in a suicide pact with her husband Paul. (As we shall see again in the next chapter, her father Karl was obsessed with pacts with the devil.) When Marx's children were in distress, they had no God to whom they could turn for forgiveness and comfort.

Some people have tried to put distance between the earlier life of Karl Marx and his later philosophy. They would insist that we should pay no attention to his beliefs and attachments until he cowrote *The Communist Manifesto* in 1848 with his friend Frederich Engels. But we must explore the demonic influences that developed early in his life and no doubt had an impact on his future philosophy.

A word of warning: As we are about to read the dark poetry that emanated out of Marx's mind, it is time for us to remember this exhortation, "Put on the whole armor of God that you might be able to stand against the schemes of the devil. For we do not wrestle against flesh and blood but against the rulers, against the authorities against the cosmic powers over this present darkness, praying at all times in the Spirit . . ." (read Eph. 6:10–20). What follows in the next chapters is not just a philosophical battle, but a battle waged against the "cosmic powers, over this present darkness."

Now we must return to his father's perceptive question: *Was his demon heavenly or Faustian?* In the following chapter we provide evidence that the answer is at hand.

CHAPTER 3

A Revolutionary in the Making

"A Man Possessed by Ten Thousand Devils!"

"With clenched and threatening fist he rages without rest,
As though ten thousand devils had seized him by the hair."[1]

Some scholars dispute whether those words were actually intended as a reference to Karl Marx, but they are embedded in a dark comedy written by Marx's partner and disciple Friedrich Engels. Speaking of a black man from Trier (you will remember that Trier is the town where Marx was born), Engels writes in part:

He stands at the corner, with glowing eyes,
He faces the world like a madman;
With clenched and threatening fist he rages without rest,
As though ten thousand devils had seized him by the hair.

He storms through street and alley, his eyes flash wild and grim,
And curses fall like thunder from his lips in furious stream;
He howls and roars and bellows until the windows shake—
The people flee in terror from the wild and raging man.[2]

Robert Payne, author of a definitive book, *Marx: A Biography* (published in 1968), writes that there is no doubt that this is a reference to Marx. Payne quotes an actual description of Marx: "His wild temper, his impetuosity, his habit of leaping upon his prey. He would clench his fist and roar interminably for the remaining forty years of his life."[3]

Marx himself tried his hand at expressing his views and beliefs through creative forms of writing. His poetry, however, appears influenced by Satan and inspired by his hatred of God. Filled with references to suicide pacts, violence, a thirst for blood, and destruction, "Fiddler," and the two poems that follow it below, were written when he was eighteen years old.

> Look now, my blood-dark sword shall stab
> Unerringly within thy soul.
> God neither knows nor honours art.
>
> The hellish vapours rise and fill my brain,
> Till I go mad and my heart is utterly changed.
> See this sword—
> the Prince of Darkness sold it to me.—
>
> For he strikes the time and gives the sign,
> Ever more boldly I play the dance of death.
>
> I must play darkly, I must play lightly,
> Until my heart and my violin burst asunder.[4]

Look carefully at these references: violent images reminiscent of Goethe's *Faust*. A blood-red sword, hellish vapors rise and fill the brain, and this line: "See this sword—the

Prince of Darkness sold it to me.—For he strikes the time and gives the sign."

When I began writing this book, I assumed Marx was an atheist. I am no longer convinced of that. It is more likely that he did indeed believe in God but hated Him and wrote about taking vengeance on the Almighty, dethroning Him and heaping Him with spite.

Consider these words:

With disdain I will throw my gauntlet
full in the face of the world,
And see the collapse of this pygmy giant
Whose fall will not stifle my ardour.

Then will I wander godlike and victorious
Through the ruins of the world
And, giving my words an active force,
I will feel equal to the Creator.[5] (Emphasis added.)

Of course, Marx claimed he did not actually believe in a Creator but used that last line as a contrast between the prevailing religious belief of his day and his own desire to be a destroyer. When I read those lines, I call to mind the words of Mephistopheles in Goethe's *Faust*: "All that has come into existence deserves to be destroyed."[6]

Another poem, "The Pale Maiden," stands as a dark testimony:

She is wringing her lily-white hands,
The tears start to her eyes;

Fire brands the bosom,
Longing consumes the heart.
Thus Heaven have I forfeited,
I know it full well.
My soul, once true to God,
Is chosen for hell.[7]

Those last four lines are chilling. What a tragic testimony of one who, as a teenager, wrote some words of adoration about Christ, but like Judas, turned against Him with anger and hate. These early poems give us information on the struggles of Marx's soul and the contempt he had for God.

Like Faust, perhaps Marx made a pact with the devil but intended to win in the end.

Communism's Demonic Influence

In his short book titled *Was Karl Marx a Satanist*?, Richard Wurmbrand, a pastor imprisoned and tortured in Romania for fourteen years for preaching the gospel, agrees that ultimately, we must leave judgments to God; but it is clear that Marx was obsessed with making pacts with the devil. Wurmbrand saw firsthand the most evil and perverse torture that Marxism brought. He would also agree with the conclusion that Marx's goal was to "wipe capitalism from the earth and God out of heaven."[8]

In his poem "Invocation of One in Despair," Marx wrote,

So a god has snatched from me my all
In the curse and rack of destiny.
All his worlds are gone beyond recall—
Nothing left for me but enmity!

I shall build my throne high overhead,
Cold, tremendous shall its summit be.
For its bulwark—superstitious dread,
For its Marshall—blackest agony.

Who looks on it with a healthy eye
Shall turn back, deathly pale and dumb,
Clutched by blind and chill Mortality,
May his happiness prepare its tomb."[9]

I've mentioned that it is common to describe Marx as a sincere man with a desire to help humanity. The influential philosopher Karl Popper, who rejected Marxism, nevertheless writes, "One cannot do justice to Marx without recognizing his sincerity. His open-mindedness, his sense of facts, his distrust of verbiage . . . [this] made him one of the most influential fighters against hypocrisy and pharisaism. He had a burning desire to help the oppressed . . ."[10]

We shall have to leave his motives for God to judge, but this much we know: Marx had a sinister (even demonic) interest that gives us deep insight into his mind. Was Marx sincere in his desire to help people or was he actually wanting to bring destruction to the world? Did Marx have a hidden agenda that is often overlooked? All we know is that when we look into the man's mind, we see a dark abyss, whereas Popper (and others still today) saw a man with a "burning desire to help the oppressed."[11]

Wurmbrand (who spoke at The Moody Church in the 1980s) was convinced that Marx and his followers were indeed beholden to Satan. As mentioned, he had firsthand experience of watching the communist leaders torture and kill people.

They delighted in killing, but more than that, they took pleasure in torturing them. The greater the pain they could inflict, the greater their delight and satisfaction.

In his book *Tortured for Christ*, Wurmbrand wrote, "I have seen Communists torturing Christians and the faces of the torturers shone with rapturous joy. They cried out while capturing Christians 'We are the Devil!'"[12] He recalls one torturer say, "I thank God, in whom I don't believe, that I have lived to this hour when I can express all the evil in my heart."[13] No wonder Wurmbrand said, "Communism is collective demon-possession."[14] And since they believed there was no God to call them into account, they could do as they pleased, savagely torturing their own people with delight.

Yet, Marx was addressing real injustices that were being tolerated in England and other countries such as Russia. We must try to understand the historical context of the ideas that brought about this state of affairs. As we'll see in the next chapter, when you suffer at the hands of other people who exploit you to become rich, you reach out for help anywhere you think you can find it. There are reasons why people can embrace radical ideologies. Perhaps they have no excuses, but they do have reasons.

CHAPTER 4

Structural Evil and the Search for a Solution

The Historical Context of the Existing Abuses

Let's not be quick to judge. If we had lived in England during the 1800s, we might have found Marxism appealing. When you are exploited by cruel taskmasters who are creating wealth for themselves, and you have no hope for your future, and those you love are dying with preventable diseases or overwork and starvation, you might be seeking a radical restructuring of a society. This is what is called systemic evil, evil not just committed by or confined to certain individuals but found in the very system of the social order (such as slavery in America or Nazism).

The Situation in England

This situation in nineteenth-century England was dire and helps us understand the origins of Marxism. In 1845, three years before *The Communist Manifesto* was written, Friedrich Engels published a book titled *The Conditions of the Working Class in England*. In it he detailed the deplorable working conditions in factories as being overcrowded, in unventilated surroundings, and with the lack of sanitation. Workers did not have job security; if they could no longer work, they had no means of earning a living and could succumb to poverty. It's no wonder the life expectancy among the proletariat was at an all-time low and their death rate skyrocketed.

Long hours, child labor, unbearable working conditions—this is what the proletariat had to endure just to live—*barely* live. They had no choice, no voice in opposing the brutal conditions in which they had to work. All that stood between them and starvation was employment, and if their jobs were lost, they and their family would face the very real possibility of starvation. In effect, for many, their only value in life was to make money for their heartless and wealthy factory and landowners. They had no safety net.

In the *Communist Manifesto*, we have a summary of what was happening: "Society as a whole is more and more splitting up into two great hostile camps, into two great classes directly facing each other—the bourgeoisie and proletariat."[1] Marx and Engels go on to explain how industrialization had made the markets for goods grow and that this expansion enabled factory owners to hire more workers and exploit them. The bourgeoisie had grown in power and had "pitilessly torn asunder the motley feudal ties that bound man to his 'natural superiors.'" In addition, the system "left no other bond between man and man than naked self-interest, than callous 'cash payment' . . . for exploitation, veiled by religious and political illusions, it [had] substituted naked, shameless, direct, brutal exploitation."[2]

Marx and Engels saw that industrialization was dividing the populace between the haves and the have-nots, and the divide was stark and growing. The workers were just an expendable commodity, of no value beyond what they contributed to helping the bourgeoisie make money. And if the workers had to quit working for whatever reason, they had no fallback plan. Marx and Engels correctly saw this was servitude of the worst possible sort.

They believed this exploitation was not a problem that could be tackled piecemeal; this evil was structural and ingrained in society. The solution needed to affect the entire country, and therefore, it necessitated a radical reordering of society. The collaborators proposed that the monetary relationship between workers, owners, and the general populace needed to be restructured; the old had to be torn down and the new built.

But England did not experience the communist revolution Marx and Engels called for. And as previously noted, in his old age, Engels admitted that the revolution was prevented by the Christian influence of men like Moody and Sankey and "the dangerous aid of the Salvation Army, which revives the propaganda of early Christianity, appeals to the poor as the elect."[3] So it was the Christians who were taught in their churches to help the poor and valued personal compassion that prevented the proletariat (the working class) from forcibly overthrowing the property and factory owners. The kind of violence and theft necessary to bring about the promised communist utopia could not take place in such a religious climate.

Since Russia was the first country to experience the radical reordering of society based on Marxism, let's go there and put ourselves in their context.

The Situation in Russia

"You Americans don't understand," my Russian interpreter said to me back in 1985 when my wife, Rebecca, and I visited both Russia and Ukraine. There, I had the privilege of preaching in some of the churches in what was then called the Soviet Union. "You don't understand the exploitation, the misery, the starvation, and the persecution we Russians endured under the tsars. Communism seemed like an experiment that needed to be tried."

He explained that as a child during the communist revolution and the final days of the reign of Tsar Nicholas II, the last tsar of Russia, he and his parents had to spend a winter hiding in a barn, wondering each day where they could find food. Yes, Lenin's Bolsheviks (leftist revolutionaries) were seen as evil, but it was believed they could not be more evil than the elites who lived in their mansions, exploiting the factory workers and demanding that the peasants give them all their grain.

Rebecca and I have visited Saint Petersburg and have seen the opulent mansions in which the tsars lived. Believing themselves to be entitled, one tsar would pass along the leadership to his child or another relative. Each tried to rule their vast empire, living lavishly in their palaces with arrogance and tightfisted ruthlessness. Nicholas II ruled from 1894 until he abdicated in 1917; a year later, he and his family were executed by the Bolsheviks. He was not capable of managing the great empire or bringing reforms. In fact, it is reported that his wife, Tsarina Alexandra, regularly visited an occultist/mystic named Grigori Rasputin, often seeking advice even for the affairs of state, which she then pressed upon her husband. The result was decisions which proved to be disastrous.

During our visit, I learned that we as Americans are indeed too quick to judge, too quick to denounce a political philosophy that promises to take ownership from wicked, entrenched exploiters and give it to the workers who, it was believed, would rule with fairness and justice. Russia would be the first major country to implement a radical political philosophy birthed in the writings of two men in England.

A Better Path Forward

Before we expound on the Marx/Engels radical solution to structural evil, we should point out that those who wanted change did have some other options open to them. In Britain, there was a government in place that could have passed legislation that would have improved, if not stopped, this type of widespread exploitation. Many years before their time, William Wilberforce (1753–1833) did not advocate for the "forceable overthrow of society" as Marx and Engels did, but worked tirelessly to end the abhorrent slave trade. Marx and Engels could have encouraged unions to lobby politicians to insist on laws that would have improved the salaries of the proletariat and addressed their working conditions.

Already, in 1833, the British government had passed the Factory Act, which prohibited the employment of children under the age of nine in factories. Laws like this, by our standards, were embarrassingly deficient, but they helped put the country on a path toward meaningful change.

Also, instead of attempting to dethrone God, Marx and Engels should have been insisting that churches increase their help and care for the poor, band together in their suffering, and press for cultural changes. They should have challenged those who professed religion to put their faith into practice and minister to the broken and the dying.

But Marx and Engels did not go in that direction; instead, they chose a revolutionary path requiring the overthrow of society. They believed they should take on the huge task of restructuring the economy in a way that would change the whole social order.

The Origin of Progressivism

Marx and Engels were influenced by the philosopher Friedrich Hegel who taught that ideas develop in history through a dialectic, namely of contradiction and resolution. As opposites resolve themselves into something new, this brings about a new dialectic, and the resulting conflict brings about the ever-changing development of ideas. Marx and Engels applied this dialectical approach to class struggles, believing that the conflicting economic disparities between the workers and the capitalists could be more quickly resolved by means of a revolution.

Their philosophy spawned what has become known as *progressivism*, the belief that change is good and necessary and always leads to something better. Although today the word is variously defined, when it is applied to Marx and Engels, it means that history is being pushed forward from one stage to another. So, resolving the conflict between the workers and the owners is necessary to bring about a better version of an ever-changing society. Just as Darwin discovered evolution in the natural world, the same principles of progress apply to class struggles fueled by economics.

To be clear, although Marx and Engels were not alone in arguing for the need to wrest ownership and power from the ruling class and give it to the underclass, they provided a philosophical framework that posited more clearly how a radical revolution would speed up the process. This ideology was seen as innovative and progressive.

Let's not lose sight of this: Marxism's appeal is that a revolution would bring about something better, giving the working man dignity, a fair wage, and a seat at the table. The disparities would be resolved and eventually the ongoing changes would usher in a utopia of sorts.

What's not to like?

But early on, opposition to their progressive ideas spread. *The Communist Manifesto*, first published in 1848, addressed this opposition in its opening sentences: "A specter is haunting Europe—the specter of Communism. All the powers of old Europe have entered into a holy alliance to exorcise this specter: Pope and Czar, Metternich and Guizot French Radicals and German police-spies."[4]

Marx and Engels took the opposition against their agenda as a positive development. This meant that Communism was already acknowledged as being in existence and its ideas were being discussed. And the *Manifesto* was written to "openly, in the face of the whole world, publish their views, their aims, their tendencies, and meet this nursery tale of the specter of Communism with a manifesto of the party itself."[5]

They begin by explaining the belief we've already described, namely that history is a history of class struggles driven by economic forces. In the middle of the Industrial Revolution, they saw the exploitation of the working class and wanted to make things better; they wanted to liberate the proletariat from the selfish wealthy landlords and factory owners who got their status and wealth at the expense of the poor hard-working laborers.[6]

Was their assessment correct?

We've already learned that their depiction of the deplorable conditions of the working class (proletariat) was essentially correct, and piecemeal approaches could not solve the problem of systemic evil. The same can be said for evils such as the slave trade and the Holocaust, which required the cooperation of a large portion of the population. Such evils could not be remedied by simply addressing abuses one by one; these evils were baked into the very fabric of the culture.

We can thank Marx and Engels for shining a spotlight on the systemic evils of society birthed in the wake of the Industrial Revolution. But we cannot thank them for the solution they proposed. We will see why their proposed solution became a curse to the world.

CHAPTER 5

The Gospel of Marxism

The Forceable Overthrow of All Existing Social Conditions

The word *gospel* in its simplest form means "good news." While it is almost always a reference to the good news of Christ's coming to redeem us, I am taking the liberty to use it for the teachings of Marx and Engels, who thought they were bringing good news to the world. If Marxism has a gospel, the following pages describe it.

While D. L. Moody was proclaiming one kind of good news to the world, explaining that Christ came to redeem us, Marx was proclaiming his version of "good news." Moody's and Marx's messages were as divergent as the east is from the west, or even heaven and hell.

Marx and Engels promoted what turned out to be six useful lies, which I have taken the liberty to call the hollow pillars of Marxism. (Exactly what made these lies so believable will be explained later in this book.)

1. When Private Property Is Abolished, Equality Will Result

Let me begin with this overarching quote from the *Manifesto*: "The theory of the Communists may be summed up in a single sentence: Abolition of private property."[1]

What are wars and conflicts about? Ownership! Ownership of the land and the means of production while the workers owned nothing and struggled to survive. The premise was: If no one owned anything, these conflicts and wars would end. Therefore, if the state owned everything, there would be no arguments as to who owned what; there would be *collective ownership*. Hence, modern Marxists like the word *collectivism*.

This means, of course, that there would be an end to individuality and freedom; the individual would be forced to blend in with the collective group; the state would be everything. The argument was that, eventually, surrendering your freedom to the state will benefit you. But in order to do that, there would have to be the elimination of bourgeois individuality, independence, and freedom—these must be destroyed.

Marx and Engels do not back down from saying that individual freedom would have to be surrendered to the greater good of the collective state. They imagine the bourgeoisie objecting to this, and so they face the objection directly: "And the abolition of this state of things is called by the bourgeois, abolition of individuality and freedom! And rightly so. The abolition of bourgeois individuality, bourgeois independence, and bourgeois freedom is undoubtedly aimed at."[2]

Don't miss their goal: *the abolition of bourgeois individuality and freedom*. Imagine that you had a store and buying and selling would not be abolished; it's just that you would not own anything that was bought or sold, rather it would be on loan from the state because everything belonged to the state. The state would control the prices, direct the commerce transactions, and control your economic decisions. Freedom and individuality will vanish in favor of the greater good of the collective. It's the price to be paid for equality of lifestyle for everyone. We return to the *Manifesto.* Marx and Engels go on to counter the anticipated reaction of opponents:

> You are horrified at our intending to do away with private property. But in your existing society, private property is already done away with for nine-tenths of the population; its existence for the few is solely due to its non-existence in the hands of those nine-tenths. You reproach us, therefore, with intending to do away with a form of property, the necessary condition for whose existence is the non-existence of any property for the immense majority of society.[3]

Note that the workers never owned private property, so it's now time for that to be true of the ruling class. After the revolution, no one will have private property and, at last, all will be equal. The writing could not be clearer. "In a word, you reproach us with intending to do away with your property. Precisely so; that is just what we intend."[4]

In their view, it would be much better if everyone worked for the state and not for themselves. The state would then "divide the spoils," so to speak, and people would not be compensated for their work, but on the basis of what they need. This would establish a "classless society." People would wake up in the morning excited to work for the state, not themselves, knowing their work would bring about shared blessings for everyone.

This is a famous line from Marx, summing up his philosophy of work: "From each according to his ability, to each according to his needs."[5] You could work hard, but it would be for other people who needed it more than you. Or you might not work hard and still insist that your needs would be met. Who was to determine what your need really was? Your definition or your neighbors'? Those questions were left unanswered.

As we shall see, this did not result in the prosperity promised for everyone. Marx apparently didn't realize that if no one *had* to work, no one would.

2. Faith in God Must Be Transferred to Faith in the State

Marx didn't just not believe in God, he *hated* God. So, of course, he wanted to shift the focus from God to the state. As he stated: "Religion is the sigh of the oppressed creature, the heart of a heartless world, and the soul of soulless conditions. It is the opium of the people."[6]

He believed religion was a panacea that kept the masses in check, and for Marx and Engels, it did so by teaching, "Yes, you are being cheated in this world, but you will be blessed in the world to come." For Marx and Engels, God was just a comfort blanket, a figment of the imagination for those who felt alienated and cheated because their blessings were postponed. Belief in the existence of God was seen as a hindrance in Marx's materialistic view of the world. Men and women have no souls that survive the death of the body; there is no God, no final judgment.

He noted that people gave money to the church—money he thought should be directed toward the state. He believed the devotion given to God must be redirected to the state. The state, not God, would give people their "daily bread."

Belief in God hampered the agenda of the new society Marx sought to develop. Economic oppression would have to be overcome by religious oppression. The deadly consequence of this can only be seen in how Marxism was applied as it spread to many countries of the world. In some countries, belief in God was outlawed; those who were found with a Bible were put to death.

3. The Family Is a Unit of Oppression That Must Be Abolished

After Marx married, he found no happiness in marriage. Marx wrote to Engels: "Blessed is he who has no family." Though quoted earlier, it bears repeating: "Every day my wife says she wishes she and the children were in their graves, and I really cannot blame her, for the humiliations, torments . . . one has to go through."[7]

In the *Manifesto*, Marx insisted on the abolition of the family. He acknowledged that there would be an outcry if this were done. But he continues, "Do you charge us with wanting to stop the exploitation of children by their parents? To this crime we plead guilty."[8] Parents exploited their children by teaching them about God and fixed morality. Marx contended that children should belong to and be educated by the state; parents could not be trusted to educate their children.

As Engels put it, "The education of all children, from the moment they can get along without a mother's care, shall be in state institutions at state expense."[9] A stay-at-home mom would be submitting to servitude. In his view, children should be educated by the state so that they would be educated about the supremacy of Communism and the dangers of belief in God.

Engels lived out this philosophy; he did not believe in marriage or the family, so he had several affairs instead. Marx himself had an affair with his housekeeper, who bore him a son. Marx denied the son was his; Engels accepted paternity of the boy and called him Henry Frederick Demuth, Freddy Engels.[10]

What were their objections to marriage and family? First, these institutions were units of oppression: men oppressed their wives, children were oppressed by their parents who took them to church, and, of course, God was the ultimate oppressor. Marriage was just another economic relationship; women stayed with their husbands not because of love, but because of need. Biblical laws such as "Thou shalt not commit adultery" were seen to simply enforce male domination and keep wives slaves to their husbands. Such laws codified "male patriarchy."

All inheritance rights had to be abolished; after all, when some children inherited their parents' wealth, this produced inequality. To use a modern baseball analogy: It was not fair that some children were born on second or third base; everyone should be born at home plate, with no more advantages than the others. The state would give each child the proper care, education, and salary so that everyone could hit a home run regardless of their work or lack of it. Equality was the goal.

In 1884, a year after Marx died, Engels wrote a book titled *The Origin of the Family, Private Property and the State*, which he said reflected both his and Marx's views of the family. Paul Kengor describes their teaching: "Private housework would be nationalized, with mothers instead being corralled into the fields and factories to do more meaningful work. Housework, from cooking to cleaning, would become a government industry, as would childcare, which would become a communal affair."[11]

This would bring deliverance from "the chains of traditional family economic bondage."[12]

But for the Marxists, it is not enough for children to be educated by the state, they must be so indoctrinated in the blessings of atheism and the Marxist ideal that they would turn against their parents if their parents believed in God or read the Bible. Children were trained to spy on their parents. Teachers were trained to ask their pupils if their parents were fully in line with the goals of the state or if they subverted the state by belief in God. Children either had to lie or to tattle on their parents, who would be severely punished if their religious convictions were evident at home.

I, personally, have been told stories by families in communist countries who say their child was forced to tell whether their parents had a Bible in their home and if they read it. Imagine children having to choose between telling the truth or seeing their parents punished or, perhaps, even killed. One woman told me that you could not trust members of your family because they would receive bribes to snitch on you. We know, in one instance, a wife secretly received bribes for reporting her husband's activities—all in the name of liberation.

4. All Belief in Transcendent Truth and Laws are Socially Constructed to Hold on to Power

Regarding what are called eternal truths, the *Manifesto* states:

> There are, besides, eternal truths, such as Freedom, Justice, etc., that are common to all states of society. But Communism abolishes eternal truths, it abolishes all religion, and all morality, instead of constituting them on a new basis; it therefore acts in contradiction to all past historical experience.[13]

Notice that Communism will not even seek to establish eternal truths on a new basis because its views represent a radical break with "all past historical experience." According to the dialectic borrowed from Hegel's philosophy, ideas are constantly in flux, so Marx and Engels concluded that yes, so-called truth did exist, but it was not static. Rather it was constantly evolving, and it will continue to evolve. Laws exist only to keep the bourgeoisie in power and could be changed as needed when the working proletariat was in charge.

Today, parents of college students often wonder why the younger generation thinks differently than they do. One reason is that many of them have been indoctrinated by Marxism, which teaches that truth is socially constructed. Progressivism has taught them that reality is constantly changing, and since there is no fixed reference point, truth is subjective and is dependent on "what it means to me." So, "you have your truth and I have my truth."

To Marx and Engels, there is no God who has given humanity universal laws; all laws and human rights are created by the state and can be taken away by the state as it sees fit. Therefore, no one has the right to even criticize the state unless the state gave them that right.

In writing this book, these words from the Declaration of Independence have taken on new meaning for me: "We hold these truths to be self-evident, that all men are created equal, that they are endowed by their Creator with certain unalienable Rights, that among these are Life, Liberty and the pursuit of Happiness."[14]

Revolutionary!

The Founding Fathers of the United States believed there were some rights the state couldn't take away. The founders knew that life, liberty, and the pursuit of happiness are gifts from God. But, of course, Communism, along with other humanistic philosophies, has always invaded the freedoms intended by God to be given to His human creation. This is state encroachment.

Why is there no freedom of expression in communist countries? Your individuality must be submerged for the greater good of the state; belief in the ideology of Communism is mandatory. Rights such as freedom of expression given by the state are rescinded by the state.

5. A Violent Revolution Is Needed to Overthrow the Existing Order and Establish the Rulership of the Working Class

This pillar is chilling.

Everyone quotes the last words of the *Manifesto*, "The proletarians have nothing to lose but their chains. . . . Workingmen of all countries, unite!"[15] But what they miss are the sentences that come just before that: "The Communists disdain to conceal their views and aims. *They openly declare that their ends can be attained only by the forcible overthrow of all existing social conditions. Let the ruling classes tremble at a Communist revolution.*"[16] (Emphasis added.)

Those words should have been enough to cause everyone to tremble. Here is a call for the violent overthrow of the whole order of society. Capitalism, the nuclear family, religion, the borders between countries, individual rights—everything is to be forcibly destroyed!

Elsewhere Marx said he would not apologize for the violence his revolution would bring. He said, "We must do everything to make the fight as violent as possible when it comes. . . . We are ruthless and ask no quarter. *When our turn comes we shall not disguise our terrorism.*"[17] (Emphasis added).

The result would be millions of people killed, shot, starved, or at the very least, deprived of goods and services. Freedom would be gone, churches closed, Bibles burned, and children educated in atheism and trained to spy on their parents. The goods and services people need would be mismanaged and the stores largely empty.

"*Let the ruling classes tremble at a Communist revolution . . .*"

Well might the world tremble.

6. Eventually, There Must Be a Borderless World

Workers "have nothing to lose but their chains. Workingmen of all countries, unite!"[18]

Marx envisioned a future where the world would be united, each country serving the other. As it is, he famously stated that "the working men have no country."[19] This reflected his belief that the proletariat transcends national boundaries and shares common interests in overcoming capitalistic exploitation.

He envisioned a communist society where concepts like "nations" and "currency" would be collective, not owned by individuals; you own nothing and yet you will be content because the state will take care of your needs. The goal is "centralization of credit in the hands of the state, by means of a national bank with state capital and an exclusive monopoly."[20] No individual bank accounts are needed because the state has an exclusive monopoly on all the wealth.

Marx believed borders create dependencies and inequalities by restricting access to resources and labor. Therefore, Marxists advocate for no borders—something that today's Socialists still vie for. One recent example of Marxist advocacy for open borders took place in 2019 at the Revolution Festival in London. Niklas Albin Svensson delivered a keynote speech titled "Why Marxists Must Fight for Open Borders." In it he said, "Revolutionaries must oppose any repression of migrants and refugees, and fight instead for workers of all countries to unite. . . . Borders are not natural; they are created by the capitalist state to keep the working class divided." Svensson ties this position directly to Marxist theory and said that the free movement of workers is necessary for global socialist unity.[21]

And so it was that, as W. Cleon Skousen put it, "Marx surveyed the world and dreamed of a day when the whole body of humanity could be forced into a gigantic social image which conformed completely to Marx's dream of a perfect society."[22] He surely knew this would result in the killing of untold multitudes, but it was the price to be paid for liberation of the world. Though the origin of the following quote is unknown, it is probably what Marx, Lenin, and Stalin believed: "The last capitalist we hang will be the one who sold us the rope."

Yes, hang the capitalists, and all will be well.

Let's see how that turned out.

CHAPTER 6

Marxism Applied: Criminals Needed

The End Justifies the Means

Thomas Sowell, an economist and social commentator, said, "Stupid people can create problems, but often it takes brilliant people to create a real catastrophe."[1] Marx and Engels were brilliant. And many of their followers chose to be blind to the fact that it was impossible for Marxist principles to actually work. Many died trying to make them work, and in the process, left behind a trail of indescribable destruction.

Let's remember the words of Mephistopheles in *Faust*, "All that has come into existence deserves to be destroyed."[2] As we have learned, Marx did not believe society could be fixed; it had to be destroyed and rebuilt on the rubble left in the wake of a revolution. Keep in mind that the Bible describes the devil as "the angel of the bottomless pit. His name in Hebrew is Abaddon, and in Greek he is called Apollyon" (Rev. 9:11). Both words mean *destroyer*.

Marx needed dedicated visionaries who would fulfill his dream of a remade world. He needed the annihilation of all opposition and the downfall of all existing governments. For this, he needed a new kind of human being.[3] He needed men who were not bound by ethics, compassion, or reason, but those who could be depended upon to do whatever was needed to construct a whole new "existing society" over the rubble of the existing one. He needed a band of angry criminals, not governed by decency, and instead, willing to make a treaty they intended to break; to lie, deceive, and kill would be expected. To quote Skousen again: "He released himself from all the confining restraints of honor and ethics which mankind has previously tried to use as a basis for harmonious human relations."[4]

There are many countries that have applied the principles of Marxism, but since Russia was the first, I'll give an all-too-brief survey. I'll also share what happened under Communism in a country I have visited twice: Albania.

Russia—A Brief Survey

Vladimir Lenin was trained as a lawyer. He graduated in 1887 from the Simbirsk Classical Gymnasium, first in his class with a perfect score in numerous areas, including religion, theology-related subjects, and history.[5] He came to prominence during a period of great unrest in Russia during World War I, causing the last of the tsars, Nicholas II, to abdicate. With Russia still fighting the Germans, and leadership of the country still being sorted out, Russia fell into chaos. Meanwhile copies of *The Communist Manifesto* had been circulating and were being read by the elites in Russia.

Several events precipitated the fall of Tsar Nicholas II and the collapse of the imperial government. For a time, a provisional government was set up but was incapable of bringing stability to a country in turmoil. With long soup lines, a collapsing economy, and millions of men dead in the midst of World War I, it was understandable that Lenin would arise, crush all leadership, and lead the country in what was believed to be a hopeful direction. The suffering Russian people could not possibly predict where Lenin would eventually lead them. They boarded a train not knowing its destination.

As for religion, Marx had said it was the opium of the people;[6] Lenin called it spiritual booze, enough to keep people drunk.[7] Religious worship was abolished and churches closed or were turned into warehouses or museums dedicated to the "superstitions" of Christianity. All of this necessitated cruelty and violence.

Lenin boasted, "I took off my cross and threw it in the rubbish bin."[8] A childhood friend, Gleb Krzhizhanovsky, wrote about that incident and recorded it a bit differently: When Lenin "perceived clearly that there was no God, he tore the cross violently from his neck, spat upon it contemptuously, and threw it away." He described Lenin as freeing himself from "religious prejudices in typical revolutionary Leninist fashion, without prolonged hesitation or timid consideration."[9]

Lenin was a brilliant organizer and believed a small group of revolutionaries could arise and bring stability to the various factions fighting against each other. He gave speeches reflecting the convictions of *The Communist Manifesto* and spoke about "the dictatorship of the proletariat" and the belief that the present situation could not be corrected, but rather those who opposed his revolution should be killed. After all, as Marx said, the vision of Socialism could only take place by the forcible overthrow of the existing society. Lenin turned the chaos in Russia into a mandate for civil war. He did what he thought he needed to do to accomplish his goals.

Rod Dreher, in his book *Live Not by Lies*, put it this way: "Marxism appealed to restless, young intellectuals who were sick of the old order, had lost faith in reforming it, and were desperate to tear the system down and replace it with something entirely different. Marxism stood for the future. Marxism stood for progress."[10] Dreher goes on to say that "Marx and his disciples replaced the Christian hope in a reward in heaven with the belief that perfection could—and inevitably would—be established on this earth, after a savage apocalypse, and through the application of science and science-based politics."[11]

In February 23, 1917, a group of women staged a demonstration for bread. Later Lenin, who knew the power of slogans, called his Bolshevik revolution a fight for "Power to the Soviets, Land to the Peasants, Peace to the Nations, Bread to the Starving!"[12] The slogan offered hope, but the promises were hollow and the end result disastrous. Nevertheless, it resonated with the people; and although there were a number of revolutionary factions, when plotting his takeover, Lenin had the intuition as to when he should let time pass and when they should proceed. When he deemed the right time had come amid a time of national turbulence, he and his band of followers gained the upper hand.

The secret police were employed to keep the people in line with Lenin's established goals. Perceived enemies were publicly hanged to strike fear into the hearts of those who opposed his leadership and were plotting his downfall. In keeping with Marx, private property in Russia was abolished, accomplished by brutal murder, ultimately of millions. Lenin's armed gangs came to towns and business and told the people that their property and possessions were no longer theirs but belonged to them as Lenin's followers. Homes were ransacked to find any hidden valuables, and those who protested were tortured or had to starve. In 1937, Joseph Stalin instituted the Great Terror where so-called show trials were used to forcibly remove dissenters from the Communist Party.

Let us remember that once the proletariat began to rule, it was not enough to stamp out all religious services, so people—primarily Christians—were forced to renounce their faith at the pain of death. As Aleksandr Solzhenitsyn so brilliantly showed in *The Gulag Archipelago*, those in charge took sadistic delight in torturing those who were perceived as disagreeing with the new orthodoxy. You did not have to say or do anything to be targeted for death; you just had to belong to the educated class or own property the ringleaders wanted.

Later, Lenin realized that in order to improve the existing economic conditions, a limited form of Capitalism had to be allowed. People were going to have to produce goods and services and even have land they could claim as their own.

Be that as it may, Lenin has gone down in history as having established the first Marxist-Socialist state: the Union of Soviet Socialist Republics or USSR. There was tight control of the people; everyone had to march in step with the new regime. Before Lenin died, he wrote a letter warning the powers that be that Joseph Stalin should not succeed him; Lenin had seen the erratic ruthlessness of Stalin and believed he would worsen the country's situation. Lenin's predictions became all too true.

Stalin instituted collective farms; the state, not the farmers themselves, made the decisions as to what should be planted; the grain that was grown was seized and sold on the open market to make money for the state. So, when famine came, there was not enough grain to feed the populace. Millions of children starved to death along with their parents. When the state took the place of God, there were no evils that were out of bounds in order to achieve the Marxist goal of tight government control. The ruling state became a haven for criminals.

"Equality Enforcers" would see to it that everyone stayed in line. The individual was expendable; group identity had to survive as best it could within the ironclad collective. Become acquainted with that word, *collectivism.*

George Santayana said, "Those who cannot remember the past are condemned to repeat it."[13] So, what can we learn from the Russian experiment? Let us remember that a small group of influential radicals can have more power than their numbers suggest. They can overwhelm a country with plausible sounding promises that prove as unworkable as saying that people can drink air. With threats, propaganda, and emotionally satisfying messages, a country can quickly descend into an abyss.

Read the words of warning from Solzhenitsyn:

> If the intellectuals in the plays of Chekhov who spent all their time guessing what would happen in twenty, thirty, or forty years had been told that in forty years interrogation by torture would be practiced in Russia; that prisoners would have their skulls squeezed within iron ring . . . that they would be trussed up naked to be bitten by ants and bedbugs . . . and that, in the luckiest possible circumstances, prisoners would be tortured

> by being kept from sleeping for a week, by thirst, and by being beaten to a bloody pulp, not one of Chekhov's plays would have gotten to its end, because all the heroes would have gone off to insane asylums.[14]

There are some lines in the above description that I deleted because they were even more grotesque and dark than those you have just read. I, personally, have read this warning several times; when a country changes course and begins down a destructive path, it can end with horror. That can happen slowly, then suddenly.

Russia would spread its newly formed Marxism to other countries. I want to turn our attention to just one more of those countries to understand how Communism metastasized.

Albania—Fascism to Communism

Come with me to Albania, a beautiful country Rebecca and I had the privilege of visiting twice. It is a country that has learned the hard way that politics—applied political theory—can either bring liberation or intolerable slavery; it can give freedom to allow the church to grow, or it can turn churches into trophies of the supposed triumph of man over God. As in Russia, cathedrals once dedicated to God and the gospel were turned into warehouses, armories, or museums. Yes, evil politicians and their policies and laws can crush the church.

The apostle Paul was the first to spread the gospel to Albania. In Romans 15:19, he writes that he preached the gospel from Jerusalem "all the way around to Illyricum," a city in Albania. Centuries passed and the country came under the influence of

European Catholicism, then in the fifteenth century, the Ottoman Turks marched into the land, making the false promise that Islam would bring liberation to the country.

Predictably, the suppression of Christianity began in earnest. Churches were replaced by mosques, and bishops and other church leaders were either killed or expelled. Christians who were allowed to live became servants of their Islamic masters. They had to pay exorbitant taxes. They could not take a Muslim to court; they could not own horses. People were bribed into converting to Islam by being told that they would receive rewards: food, cattle, land, and other necessities. Even today, Albania considers itself to be about 70 percent Muslim; for the most part, they are tolerant of Christianity, although Muslim influence continues to expand.

But for centuries under the heavy hand of Islam, the beleaguered people were ready to turn anywhere for help. So, as World War II began, many of the people welcomed Italy's influence into their country, hoping to benefit from promises of expanding the use of their national resources and usher Albania into the modern world.

In 1939, Mussolini, leader of the Fascist Italian Empire, came to Albania to add the country to the empire. The Italians came to Albania with a message of liberation from Islamic oppression and economic hardship: Join the Italian Empire and you will benefit; we are here to help you! Of course, in reality, the Fascists didn't care about the people; they were there to exploit the country's natural resources and force the people to serve their expansionist cause. The people were under new oppressors who saw the country only as fodder for Mussolini and his henchmen.

But the Italian Empire collapsed in 1943 and surrendered to the Allies. This was followed by the occupation of Nazi forces who claimed to establish the Albanian Kingdom. But soon this was opposed by partisan Communists within Albania who rose up to oppose the power of the pro-Nazi puppet government. Because the communist uprising was inspired from within the country, Communism seemed to be the best means to establish a sense of independence and national control. The Communists offered many promises: prosperity, economic equality, and an end to the terrible abuses workers experienced. This was advertised as a workers' movement. Remember what Karl Marx said: "Working men of all countries, unite!"

We've learned that the thesis of Marxism is: Change the environment and you change the man. Or we could put it this way: Lift the oppression and people will live in freedom, prosperity, and with joy. After all, human nature is perfectible and your needs would be met. "From each according to his ability, to each according to his needs."[15]

But as we have learned, in order to establish communist rule, religion had to be suppressed. To enforce that, communist dictator Enver Hoxha criminalized all religion; churches and mosques were closed. In addition, the most horrid forms of persecution began. There is a museum in Tirana that I visited that provides the details of the brutal murders of many pastors, priests, and Muslim leaders. Decades after Hoxha's death in 1985, mass graves were uncovered where the skeletons of people were still chained together. According to the BBC, under Hoxha, an estimated 200,000 people passed through the regime's Gulag-modeled labor camps, and more than 6,000 went missing. "Nearly all the missing people are believed to have been executed or died of neglect or torture in the camps. Many were political prisoners, suspected of opposition to the regime."[16]

Imagine if you were taken to court and you had to swear allegiance to the brutal President Enver Hoxha whose picture hung prominently behind the desk of the judge. Of course, these were show trials, where guilt was established not on the basis of what you did, but by the excuse of the state to have you tortured and eliminated. For example, if you owned land that the criminals who ruled the country wanted, you were taken to court and found guilty of conspiring against the state. If the sentence was death, you would be tortured then killed. The communist grip on Albania made it the "North Korea" of its time.

In 1967, there was a declaration that Albania was officially an atheist country. Hoxha determined to rid the country of every vestige of Christianity.

> The authorities conducted a violent campaign to extinguish religious life in Albania, claiming that religion had divided the Albanian nation and kept it mired in backwardness. Students [joined] agitators [who] combed the countryside, forcing Albanians to quit practicing their faith. Despite complaints, even by APL [Party of Labour of Albania] members, all churches, mosques, monasteries, and other religious institutions had been closed or converted into warehouses, gymnasiums, and workshops by year's end.[17]

In May of that year, institutions of every religion were forced to hand over a total of 2,169 churches, mosques, cloisters, and shrines. Many of these former places of worship were converted into cultural centers for Albanian youth.

> The clergy were publicly vilified and humiliated, their vestments taken and desecrated. Many Muslim mullahs and Orthodox priests buckled under and renounced their "parasitic" past. More than 200 clerics of various faiths were imprisoned, others were forced to seek work in either industry or agriculture, and some were executed or starved to death. The cloister of the Franciscan order in Shkodër was set on fire, which resulted in the death of four elderly monks.[18]

One literary monthly reported the event, stating that the youth had "'created the first atheist nation in the world.'"[19]

In the booklet *The Battle for Albania*, Albanian missionaries Edwin Jacques and David Young write: "A large number of religious leaders were interned, imprisoned or executed, often being charged with collaboration with the Fascist occupiers."[20] Before people were killed, they were publicly humiliated. As the pastors and priests were marched down the streets, they were often beaten and had excrement thrown at them.

Imagine that in order to "liberate" people, the Communists had to destroy their religious beliefs and oppress any who dared have a Bible. They believed that *the way you get rid of oppression is to oppress anyone who disagrees with the orthodoxy of the state.*

Jacques and Young quote from the book *Scientific Atheism*, which says,

> We Albanians are studying the new theories which are denying God. We fight with scientific atheistic materialism against all belief in God. In this way we clear the path of religious

> rubbish to pave the way for the ideological revolution. This powerful war against God is the unshakeable task of Marxism–Leninism. It shapes the education and forming of the new man. Religion is a constant opium that never stops: for a believer it is negative emotion; false happiness—a joy without taste—a food of fresh air. God is our greatest enemy.[21]

Scientific Atheism goes on to say that the aim is to liberate people from religious bondage and that atheism is their reason for living. Read the next quotation: "What Hitler, Stalin, Mao Tse-Tung and all other dictators failed to achieve has been accomplished by Enver Hoxha. We have closed down all churches and mosques."[22]

In 1976, Christians were given until the end of the year to change the name of their children to names acceptable to the reigning ideological laws of the land. In other words, any biblical names such as Paul, John, Peter, etc., had to be changed. There could be no traces of Christian influence left in the land. No religious references were allowed at funerals or weddings. Many Christians burned their New Testaments for fear of being found with one. Missionaries report that they took plastic bags and filled them with Albanian New Testaments and sent them floating down the Vjosa river, hoping that if some Christians still existed in the country, they would find the bags and have copies of the Bible. Christianity was, for all intents and purposes, stamped out.

Thankfully, the revolution in 1990–1992 freed Albania from the yoke of Communism. When I was preaching in Albania a few years ago, an elderly woman came to the church with a Bible that had survived the purges. She and a few others gathered to pray and read the Word of God together during those evil days. The picture that was taken of the two of us with her Bible is one of the most memorable in my possession.

What was Communism's rationale for destroying all personal freedom? They believed that the masses had been brainwashed and there was no hope for them to understand the true communist vision. Such people had to be eliminated; and now the task of Communism was to brainwash a new generation that had the correct vision of what this world would become once Communism was fully implemented.

Most of the time, those who say politics is not important are people in the West who live under democracies; if they had lived in Albania, Russia, and the like, they would have discovered that politics is very important. As a friend of mine asks, "Have you noticed that there is no First Baptist Church in North Korea?" Leaders make laws; and those laws determine what their citizens can or cannot do. Laws can close churches, kill dissidents, and burn Bibles—laws can normalize evil and punish good.

Whether it is Nebuchadnezzar, Hitler, Stalin, Mao, or a long list of similar rulers, the end is always the same: People are forced to set aside their own personal beliefs and freedoms and march according to the beliefs of the state. The dictator must always have his way; there can be no compromise. No independent thought allowed. The sheep must follow their shepherd all the way into the abyss.

To Summarize Marxist Socialism

Economist George Reisman argues that Marxist Socialism is "a massive act of theft—the means of production must be seized from its owners and turned over to the state."[23] Such theft, of course, necessitates massive violence. Of course, in this piece Reisman does not distinguish between a democratic form of Socialism, which in our day is seen as distinct from Marxism (this distinction will be made more clearly in the chapter on Democratic Socialism). But since in the *Communist Manifesto* Marx uses the terms interchangeably, Reisman continues:

> It is because of their terror, and their desperate need to crush every breath even of potential opposition, that the rulers of socialism do not dare to allow even purely cultural activities that are not under the control of the state. For if people so much as assemble for an art show or poetry reading that is not controlled by the state, the rulers must fear the dissemination of dangerous ideas. Any unauthorized ideas are dangerous ideas, because they can lead people to begin thinking for themselves and thus to begin thinking about the nature of socialism and its rulers.[24]

Of course, Communism breaks the eighth commandment, "Thou shalt not steal." I've said this before, but Communism preaches that forceable theft, intimidation, and violence need to be used to eliminate oppression. No matter how evil it became, its defenders kept promoting it. Whether its basic ideas worked or not, the true believers kept insisting on its implementation. They did not lose sight of the idea of the utopian vision and wanted it exported to other countries. Even if it didn't work, they believed that it *should* work.

CHAPTER 7

Marxism Comes to America

The Transformation of Culture

In order for Marxism to flourish in America, it had to evolve. The revolution in Russia, with its mass purges, was not a good advertisement for the Marxist cause. It would have to be rebranded for Western audiences. It had to adapt to make it more appealing. It would have to be brought in incrementally, gradually, and without fanfare.

In Italy, there was a brilliant Marxist named Antonio Gramsci, who was imprisoned by Mussolini because he feared that Gramsci's leadership in the Communist Party was a threat to his brand of Fascism. Although Communism and Fascism share much in common, they do have differences. Both are totalitarian, that is, leaders rule over their citizenry with tight-fisted control; all things are subsumed under the state. As Mussolini put it, "Everything in the State, nothing outside the State, nothing against the State."[1] Marx agreed.

But they have this difference: Marx was primarily interested in dividing humanity against itself using economic disparities; Marxism was based on class warfare. Fascism, however, is motivated by a fervent nationalism. In this regard, it shared a great deal with Hitler's Nazi Germany.

While in prison, Gramsci pondered how Marxism could be implemented in the United States; he was disappointed that the workers in America were not rebelling to overthrow the ruling capitalist government, so he knew that Marxism would have to be implemented slowly, little by little, without a violent overthrow of the existing conditions. This would become known as "Cultural Marxism."

Gramsci saw three roadblocks to Marxism in America: Christianity, the nuclear family, and Capitalism. These three enemies would have to be toppled to eventually bring the Marxist paradise to America. The values of Christianity with its objective belief in morality would not allow the kinds of evil needed to steal land by killing and destruction. Christianity had brought with it a conservative culture—belief in God had spawned parents who passed their faith on to their children, and this was not conducive to the Marxist cause. Gramsci still kept in mind the end goal of a revolution in economics, but the road to that goal needed to be carefully orchestrated.

He said, "Socialism is precisely the religion that must kill Christianity."[2] In order to accomplish this, Socialism had to deal with the education system and media to transform the consciousness of society. Regarding the school system, Gramsci wrote, "The history of education shows that every class which has sought to take power has prepared itself for power by an autonomous education. . . . Popular schooling should be placed under the control of the great workers' unions."[3] In other words, parental rights should be superseded by unions that would be more favorable to the eventual Marxist goal.

He also knew that his goal of "killing" Christianity meant

that controlling the media was not just important, it was necessary. "The press is the most dynamic part of the ideological structure of the dominant classes. . . . A newspaper (or a group of newspapers, or a type of newspaper, or journalism in general) is the point of contact between the masses and the ruling group in the most immediate and continuous way."[4] Under Communism, the media would have to be nationalized, so that only the "correct" ideology would be promoted to the masses.

Read this carefully: Gramsci also believed that Socialism could be spread by the church. The religious revolutionist should be able to take Scripture passages that warn against money and materialism and reinterpret them into modern socialist language.

Gramsci said,

> In Italy, the Catholic religion has been (and continues to some extent to be) one of the elements that constitute the national-popular "common sense." It is therefore necessary to take this fact into account in the work of moral and intellectual reform. One should stress the practical importance that the Catholic worker or peasant can attribute to certain evangelical phrases or parables (for example, "it is easier for a camel to pass through the eye of a needle than for a rich man to enter the kingdom of heaven," or "the last shall be first," or "blessed are the poor," etc.). These phrases can be used politically to obtain certain mass effects, to create bonds of solidarity, to arouse feelings of justice and equity even in very backward strata. A socialist who knows how to use them intelligently—without falling into the hybridism of "Christian socialism" or into demagogic opportunism—can achieve very positive results in

> the work of moral and intellectual reform. *It is a question of translating the religious language into historical-political language, of showing how the same aspirations that Christianity places in the beyond can be realized on earth through the collective action of men.*[5] (Emphasis added.)

Don't miss it: Turn religious language into historical-political language and cancel heaven above in favor of heaven below! We could say, shift the focus from "up yonder" to what we could call "the coming Marxist paradise"! And in this way, churches could participate in the long-term Marxist agenda. And sadly, some churches have done just that.

In America, the category of oppressor vs. oppressed could not be applied to the property owners vs. the workers; that was not a major concern in the country. There would have to be a different oppressor/oppressed relationship if Marxism would incrementally take "the long march through the institutions,"[6] as Rudi Dutschke called it. Gramsci's ideas would be primarily filtered through the schools, monetary policy, media, and entertainment, and thus seep into the culture, eventually bringing about the desired revolution. In effect, the Marxist motto could have been, "Destroy Christianity and its culture, and then destroy capitalism to bring in an established state-owned economic system." He believed that if a minority in key positions of leadership grasps the benefits of Communism, they would be able to convince the larger majority that they also should adopt its philosophy. Today we call this "cultural hegemony."

Calling themselves the "Institute for Social Research," Marxist thinkers met in Frankfurt, Germany, in 1923 to discuss how radical progressive ideas could be mainstreamed in the Western world, especially the United States. Writer Al Benson Jr. explains that its mission is to "criticize every pillar of Western culture—family, democracy, common law, freedom of speech, and others. The hope was that these pillars would crumble under the pressure."[7]

With the rise of Nazism, the Institute moved to Columbia University in New York in 1934, where these ideas became mainstream in many of America's educational institutions. The goal: to find classes of victims who would be angry and ready to become involved in social action; or more accurately, social destruction. Among this group was Herbert Marcuse, who immigrated from Germany to join these Marxists at Columbia to discuss the ongoing infiltration of Marxism into America. (Remember that name because I will refer to him later in this chapter.)

These efforts could disrupt the culture and bring about conditions that would open the door for a more Marxist approach to culture. This is where "critical theory" had its beginnings, critiquing topics such as gender issues, the deconstruction of texts and documents, and economic inequality under the broad category of social justice. The intention of critical theory is to seek all the hidden agendas of power to find who is responsible and who is to blame for any power imbalances. History must be rewritten and the emphasis put on blaming and condemning everything deemed to be American. And when multiple forms of oppression are discovered, this is known as "intersectionality."

Rod Dreher writes:

> Social justice cultists are utopians who believe that the ideal of Progress requires smashing all the old forms for the sake of liberating humanity. Unlike their Bolshevik predecessors, they don't want to seize the means of economic production but rather the means of cultural production. They believe that after humanity is freed from the chains that bind us—whiteness, patriarchy, marriage, the gender binary, and on and on—we will experience a new and radically improved form of life.[8]

Let me be quick to point out that we as Christians should fight for justice based on biblical principles. As the prophet Micah put it so clearly, "He has told you, O man, what is good; and what does the LORD require of you but to do justice, and to love kindness, and to walk humbly with your God?" (Mic. 6:8). But when justice is divorced from truth it becomes whatever people want it to be; it divides and seeks conflict, not reconciliation and a message of cooperation and hope. The prophet Isaiah described what happens when justice and righteousness are based on a humanistic standard: "Justice is turned back, and righteousness stands far away; for truth has stumbled in the public squares, and uprightness cannot enter. Truth is lacking, and he who departs from evil makes himself a prey" (Isa. 59:14–15). The Israelites in the book of Judges did whatever was right (just) in their own eyes (see Judg. 21:25). So-called justice that is not based on truth leads to an unbridled disaster.

What follows are a few of those attacks from those who have participated either knowingly or unknowingly in the slow Marxist march "through the institutions." I have dealt with these issues much more thoroughly in my books *We Will Not Be Silenced* and *No Reason to Hide*.[9]

Rewrite the Past to Control the Future

Read these two prescient quotes from George Orwell: "The most effective way to destroy people is to deny and obliterate their own understanding of their history,"[10] and "Who controls the past controls the future: who controls the present controls the past."[11]

Communism has always sought to give the impression that when it takes over, the nation has a new beginning. The past has to be vilified and discussed only to point out its evils in order to give legitimacy to the new way forward. When Communism came to Russia, monuments of the past were destroyed, streets were renamed, and Saint Petersburg became Leningrad, and later, Stalingrad. Other cities also were renamed. Under Mao Zedong (also Tse-tung), leader of the communist revolution in China, the break with the past was even more dramatic. Nations had to be cleansed from their past as the new day of Communism dawned.

Keep in mind that today's radical left agrees that America cannot be fixed, it must be destroyed, and on the rubble of the past, a new beginning must be erected that will be free of all of abuses and disparities of the past. Thus, our Founding Fathers must be vilified, the Constitution must be "deconstructed," and all of American history must be interpreted through the lens of slavery, racism, and the destructive influence of "white privilege."

Arthur Schlesinger, a historian and former confidant to President John F. Kennedy, observed, "History is to the nation much as memory is to the individual. The individual who loses his memory doesn't know where he came from or where he's going and he becomes dislocated and disoriented."[12] I might add that a person who has lost his memory can be manipulated into believing he is whomever someone else says he is.

Visualize yourself stepping out of the door of a rather impressive eighteenth-century. building and walking along the street. When you look back, you can clearly see where your trip originated. But suppose you turn a corner, and when you look back, you see a twenty-first-century building bearing no resemblance to where you came from. Radical secularists insist we turn a corner so that we will lose sight of the Judeo-Christian influence of our past; but if we do look back, they want us to see our religious history as a bane, not a blessing. They want us to substitute a modern worldview in the place of our religious sixteenth-century roots.

Several years ago, the editors at *The New York Times Magazine* completed a project that sought to "reframe" America's history to mark 1619 as the year of its true founding. This is when the first slaves arrived in Jamestown, which the project puts forth as the central event in the founding of America. They concluded that slavery is foundational to America's beginning, and along with it came the plantation and the beginning of Capitalism.

According to *The New York Times Magazine*, these two evils show that "our democracy's founding ideals were false when they were written."[13] In other words, the authors of the Declaration of Independence, who wrote that "all men are created equal and endowed by our Creator with certain unalienable Rights,"[14] did not believe what they were writing.

The creator of the project, journalist Nikole Hannah-Jones, wrote an essay in 1995 in which she said "the white race is the biggest murderer, rapist, pillager, and thief of the modern world." The white race is made up of "barbaric devils, bloodsuckers and Columbus was no different than Hitler."[15] Clearly the project she oversaw was intended to reflect her beliefs.

Is this a fair or accurate reading of American history? Slavery is an abomination. I have read stories about the slave trade that would cause a stone to weep. No person should own another, and America's history of buying and selling slaves should be documented and denounced in all of its horrible aspects. And most certainly, the black community knows the continuing impact of slavery in their history. It is important for us to listen carefully to their stories and pursue unity. The gospel gives us the tools to both rightly denounce sin and to seek unity through forgiveness and reconciliation in Christ.

Yet, we should not be surprised that the Founding Fathers had slaves; what should surprise us is that they wrote documents that they knew would be used to fight slavery. But any such balance cannot be allowed when the past is rewritten to change our history in order to adjust to a different history altogether. Sadly, there are those who believe that all of our history must be poured through the prism of the worst of our history; they cannot honestly say there is something good that has come from America.

A cardinal rule among the radical left is to never compare America with other countries. If you do that, America will look too good. Rather, compare it with its high ideals. And because America is not perfect and never will be, the good America has done will always be discounted when the focus is on its many failures.

Once again, Orwell had it right, "The past was erased, the erasure was forgotten, the lie became truth."[16]

Use Diversity to Divide and Destroy

"We are not called to *fix* problems! We are here to *use* them!"

Through the providence of God, I met a man who had been a coworker of Saul Alinsky, the community organizer in Chicago during the sixties and seventies. He told me, "We had plans as to how to help the under-resourced communities of Chicago, but Alinsky blocked them." Alinksy wanted to apply principles of Marxism to the race conflicts in the city. Yes, he saw racism as a problem to *use*.

Who was Saul Alinsky?

He is the man who wrote the book *Rules for Radicals*, in which he praised Lucifer on the opening page. He writes:

> Lest we forget at least an over-the-shoulder acknowledgment to the very first radical; from all our legends, mythology, and history (and who is to know where mythology leaves off and history begins—or which is which), the first radical known to man who rebelled against the establishment and did it so effectively that he at least won his own kingdom—Lucifer.[17]

Alinsky saw that Karl Marx's principles of the oppressed vs. oppressor could be applied to race. This meant we should no longer see ourselves as individuals but rather as part of a group; a group clearly divided between white and black. You don't have to do a single thing to be an oppressor; you just have to belong to a certain class. So, the intention was not to bring harmony to the races to work together mutually, but rather to keep the races antagonistic toward each other. The goal was not to help; it was to exploit the differences. The Black/White divide was seen as an ongoing struggle necessary for the oppressed to overthrow their oppressors.

When I became senior pastor of The Moody Church in January 1980, the goal was "racial reconciliation." We tried to understand the terrible injustices of slavery, and we taught that we all must bow before the cross of Christ, working together for the good of all communities in Chicago. We rejoiced that every Sunday morning, we had people from more than seventy countries of origin, and thankfully that is still true today. After all, in heaven there will be a "great multitude that no one could number, from every nation, from all tribes and peoples and languages, standing before the throne and before the Lamb" (Rev. 7:9).

But with time, I noticed that the mood of the country was shifting; the goal was no longer racial reconciliation but racial division: We were into blaming and even shaming. Books like *White Fragility* were widely read, a book that teaches we must use racism to fight racism; it teaches that all white people are racists. Examples of "whiteness" in the United States include "individualism, the superiority of capitalism as an economic system and democracy as a political system, consumerism as a desirable lifestyle, and meritocracy (anyone can succeed if he or she works hard)."[18]

Remember, Marxism's goal is never to come together, it is to enter a state of instability and continual conflict and chaos with the hope that utopia will eventually arise. Guilt or innocence is determined by the class one belongs to. One group is always the villain; the other group is always the victim. No matter what you have done, you are judged by the class you belong to, not the good you have accomplished.

Gone was the vision of Martin Luther King, Jr.: "I have a dream that my four little children will one day live in a nation where they will not be judged by the color of their skin but by the content of their character."[19] The insertion of a Marxist understanding of this world would seek to destroy such commonsense individuality.

What does the Bible say? The New Testament was written at a time when hostility between the Jews and the Greeks (whom the Jews called barbarians) was at an all-time high. These were ethnicities that had no natural ability to bond well. Yet, they could come together because of the work of Christ.

We read in Colossians 3:11: "Here [in Christ] there is not Greek and Jew, circumcised and uncircumcised, barbarian, Scythian, slave, free; but Christ is all, and in all." The apostle Paul is not saying that Greeks become Jews or that a Scythian becomes Greek, he is saying there is a transcendent unity in Christ binding us together. We bow at the foot of the cross and then ask, *What can we do for our under-resourced neighborhoods, and how can we work toward common goals of true justice and fairness? How do we move forward, working toward a more hopeful future while acknowledging the injustices of the past?*

The church has often failed to demonstrate that unity; our goal should be to come together rather than be torn apart. Yes, of course, there are failures and, yes, the seeds of racism exist in every human heart, not just in one group of people. But the various ethnicities should not antagonize each other; rather, they should work together to bring about both fairness and justice. Thank God there are many churches here in the city of Chicago that are doing just that.

It has been correctly said that Critical Race Theory tears apart what Jesus died to bring together.

The Abolition of the Family

As we have seen, Marx, and later Gramsci, believed that poverty is the result of the oppression of the underclass, and one of the ways to do away with this oppression was to destroy the family. The family was deemed to be "class mentality" and an arrangement to keep women in line for economic and social reasons. "'Thou shalt not commit adultery' [is] said to have been created to implement the idea that . . . the wife was strictly private property belonging to [the husband]."[20] So, in Marx's mind, the destruction of the family would help bring about the economic freedom we all long for. Fathers and mothers would be able to pursue their own interests, and the bourgeois family would vanish as a matter of course, and with it, Capitalism.

Thus, we know that often here in America, the schools want to either ignore the parents' authority or insist that as teachers and professors they have superior insight into the kind of moral teaching children really need. We've heard much about the kind of aberrant sexual teaching in many of our schools that often pits the child against the parents and invites children to explore various forms of sexuality. In the media, there are many other attacks against the family in our culture.

But will the destruction of the family result in economic equality and freedom? Or is the opposite true, namely, that the family is our best hope for economic and social stability? The Bible teaches and history verifies that the family is the most essential unit of society. And often the existence of an economic underclass is the result of the internal issues *within* the families of a nation. In other words, *the destruction of the family does not bring economic stability but destroys it.*

Psychiatrist Theodore Dalrymple's book *Life at the Bottom —The Worldview That Makes the Underclass*, shows that the most powerful influence relegating people to the underclass is moral issues. For the record, Dalrymple's father was a Communist. Dalrymple himself is an atheist but argues that socially liberal progressive views minimize individual responsibility and produce an underclass afflicted by violence, sexually transmitted disease, welfare dependency, and drug use.

So, what causes a permanent underclass? He says,

> Of nothing is this [social pathology] more true than the system of sexual relations that now prevails in the underclass, with the result that 70 percent of the births in my hospital are now illegitimate (a figure that would approach 100 percent if it were not for the presence in the area of a large number of immigrants from the Indian subcontinent).[21]

According to him, the foremost perpetrator of the underclass is uncommitted sexual relations. People from the Indian subcontinent (the area of south central Asia) get married, stay together, get an education, and work hard so most are not part of the underclass. Dalrymple continues:

> The connection between this loosening [of morals] and the misery of my patients is so obvious that it requires considerable intellectual sophistication (and dishonesty) to be able to deny it. The climate of moral, cultural, and intellectual relativism—a relativism that began as a mere fashionable plaything for intellectuals—has been successfully communicated to those least able to resist its devastating practical effects.[22]

I suspect that immorality, sexual freedom, unmarried teenage parents, along with opioid and other addictions such as alcoholism and gambling, will always ensure that we have what Dalrymple called a "permanent underclass," and it will include all races, cultures, and ethnicities that will not face the internal moral issues holding them captive to their plight.

My point: The existence of strong families is our best hope for economic stability and social advancement. It is not always true as Marxists teach that "the poor are poor because the rich are rich." But with the ongoing sexual revolution we can only expect more brokenness and with it more poverty.

In the midst of this heartache the church must step up to the plate and be the church. The church can do what social programs cannot. I greatly admire those pastors in our most under-resourced communities here in Chicago (and other cities) who are in the trenches, working with families and sharing resources and gospel ministries to give hope to people trapped in cycles of poverty and utter despair. And I'm thankful for those Christian ministries teaching children to honor marriage and have a positive image of what a family can be. And with God's help, we should stand with them with our financial help and encouragement.

God forbid that Marx's and Gramsci's vision of the abolition of the family would continue to accelerate on our watch.

The Abolition of Free Speech

Welcome to the cancel culture.

Let's begin with the Marxist philosopher Herbert Marcuse (whom I mentioned earlier). He was a part of the Frankfurt Institute for Social Research and came to America to teach at Columbia University. I remember having discussions about him back in the 1960s. He attributed all the evils of society to Capitalism, believing that a few wealthy elites controlled the means of production. The workers who supported the capitalists worked harder than they needed to; knowingly or unknowingly, they were simply feeding the greed of the capitalists.

Marxism, he believed, would remedy these inequities. But how is Marxism to be brought about? Not by freedom of speech, which he said "is loaded and dominated by existing elites, who skew the debate to favor their position."[23] According to this view, there is no level playing field because the capitalists have the advantage of deluding the masses with their rhetoric. This has resulted in violence, racism, and oppression of various kinds. As long as free speech survives, people will lack the discernment to know what is really true.

What is to be done?

Marcuse lamented, "Tolerance is extended to policies, conditions, and modes of behavior which should not be tolerated because they are impeding, if not destroying, the chances of creating an existence without fear and misery"[24] (that is, the utopian Marxist state).

To put his point simply: Freedom of speech allows capitalists to stay in power; therefore, freedom of speech should not be tolerated. To allow non-Marxists free speech is to delay, if not impede, the possibility that Marxism will prevail.

What restrictions should be placed on free speech, according to Marcuse?

> They [the restrictions] would include the withdrawal of toleration of speech and assembly from groups and movements which promote aggressive policies, armament, chauvinism,

> discrimination on the grounds of race and religion, or which oppose the extension of public services, social security, medical care, etc.[25]

So, if you believe in armaments (patriotism) and oppose same-sex marriage on religious grounds, or for that matter differ about political issues such as social security and the like, you are not entitled to free speech to defend your views. Once Marxism is firmly in place, freedom may be restored but some restrictions will continue. He writes:

> Moreover, the restoration of freedom of thought may necessitate new and rigid restrictions on teachings and practices in the educational institutions which, by their very methods and concepts, serve to enclose the mind within the established universe of discourse and behavior.[26]

What should we conclude?

Jeffery A. Tucker, editorial director at the American Institute for Economic Research, comments: "Marcuse says that if you oppose policies like social security or Obamacare, you should be denied the freedom of speech and assembly. You should be shut up and beat up. The path toward true freedom is through massive real-world oppression. *If you have the wrong views, you have no rights.*"[27] (Emphasis added.)

Let's recap. Marcuse was frustrated that Marxism had not yet prevailed and so he blamed capitalistic opposition. Therefore, capitalists had to be denied freedom of speech. Tucker, with just a hint of sarcasm, comments, "Given that he and his friends are part of a priesthood of truth, shouldn't they just be declared the winners and contrary views suppressed?"[28]

After all, as Marcuse said, "Suppression of the regressive ones [policies and opinions] is a prerequisite for the strengthening of the progressive ones."[29]

What about liberalism that always championed freedom? Marcuse writes that we must put an end to "the liberal creed of free and equal discussion." We must be "militantly intolerant."[30] Liberalism's policy of freedom of speech must be denounced.

We should be *militantly intolerant*!

Who should make the distinction between the progressive views of Marxism and the repressive views of Capitalism? The answer is the properly enlightened intellectuals like Marcuse and his friends. Marcuse describes the person who should decide who is permitted to speak as someone who is "in the maturity of his faculties as a human being."[31]

Did you get that? Those of us who aren't Marxists are immature; it follows that the ones who determine what can and can't be said are those who have maturity of their faculties. Let me say it again: Marcuse believed that Marxists should have freedom of speech, but capitalists should not. Marxists are mature thinkers; therefore, we should not argue with them. But what this means is when the Marxists speak, they want only to hear the echo of their own voice.

Ideas have consequences.[32]

Most of the faculty and students at our universities have probably never read Herbert Marcuse. But his influence has worked its way into academia just as he proposed. To quote Jeffrey Tucker one more time, "It doesn't mean that people are literally reading Marcuse or even that their professors have done so. Philosophy works this way. Bad ideas are like termites: you can't entirely see them and suddenly the whole house falls in."[33]

Tucker is right. Repressive termites are everywhere in academia, allowing only for "progressive ideas." Just think of how difficult (often impossible) it is to have a conservative speak at one of our universities. We humbly acknowledge that Herbert Marcuse won the argument. And he used free speech to do it.

Now I want to introduce you to Stanley Fish, author of *There's No Such Thing as Free Speech, and It's a Good Thing, Too.* He says:

> Individualism, fairness, merit—these three words are continually in the mouths of our up-to-date, newly respectable bigots who have learned that they need not put on a white hood or bar access to the ballot box in order to secure their ends.[34]

Reread that if you have to. Those of us who believe in free speech are compared to the Ku Klux Klan and called bigots. Stephen R. C. Hicks, who opposes such reasoning, sums up what Marcuse is saying, "So in order to equalize the power imbalance, explicit and forthright double-standards are absolutely and unapologetically called for in the postmodern Left."[35]

Double standards are absolutely and unapologetically called for. If Marx could speak from his grave in his native German, he would say, "Jawohl!"

Approved Violence

A few months after the assassination of Charlie Kirk on September 10, 2025, his organization, Turning Point USA, had a rally planned at UC Berkeley. Antifa, a radical leftist group that does not believe in free speech, turned the campus into what some called "a war zone." The sold-out TPUSA event drew protestors who lobbed smoke bombs, bottles, and fireworks, attempting to disrupt the meeting. Rioters broke through police barricades, and many were injured in the melee.

Why?

Quite simply, the radical left agrees with Marxists: Free speech should not be allowed unless it is consistent with the radical agenda. I'm reminded of the profound words of Frederick Douglass, a slave turned statesman, "[Free speech] is the great bulwark against tyranny."[36] He believed that freedom of speech had the power to put an end to slavery. No doubt Antifa disagrees that we should allow free speech; "Free speech for me, but not for thee!"

Why didn't the radical left at Berkeley not hold their own rally the next day and counter the views of TPUSA? The reason is at hand: When you are out of arguments, even in a free country, you turn to violence. The radical left can only move forward with *uncontested dominance*.

But one way to bring about the Marxist vision of utopia is to vote it in; remember, do it incrementally, do it even through democracy. There are ways to bring about the desired result without tearing everything down.

We now turn to that.

CHAPTER 8

Democratic Socialism: Marxism Lite

Sell It as a Noble Cause

The dream is free—the hustle is sold separately."

Those are the words I saw on a T-shirt recently. Democratic Socialists have dreams that can only exist in the imagination. The dreams are attractive, motivating, hopeful, and progressive. The dreams are free, but their implementation is billed separately. Yet Democratic Socialism can be sold as a noble cause: Just present the dream and don't be too concerned about the cost. The dream alone sells.

Democratic Socialism can be variously defined, but its basic philosophy is that the state must take a greater role in centralizing the economy to bring about a fairer version of income equality. It rejects the individualism of Capitalism and seeks collectivism where individuals must share their resources for the good of the whole. It may or may not eventually result in full-blown Marxism. In the section that follows, its promises and results will be clarified.

The Appeal of Marxist Socialism

This is why Marxist Socialism is so appealing.

First, it purports to care for the poor, to "help the little guy" by making the playing field level for everyone. It is sold through attractive slogans: End Poverty! Free Daycare! Free College! Free public transportation! Make goods and services more affordable! We need a government that serves all the people, not just the wealthy! Let Wall Street become Main Street! We need a universal basic income!

Who doesn't want to end poverty? Or make goods and services more affordable? These goals can even be couched in terms that appeal to Christians. We should all care about the poor, the marginalized, and the forgotten. We as Christians should give "voice to the voiceless" and stand up for those who suffer injustice in the workplace. Caring about the poor is a theme that runs throughout Scripture. Proverbs 19:17 comes to mind: "Whoever is generous to the poor lends to the LORD, and he will repay him for his deed."

Christians should take as our example the story of the Good Samaritan. He didn't ask the wounded man about his race or whether he was legal or illegal, he just saw someone in need of help and did what he could to help him. May we do the same.

The goals of Marxism appear to be "Christian," but as we shall see, the implementation of those goals through state control cannot work efficiently or effectively. The slogans are attractive but make the realization of the dream impossible. And long term, it is destructive.

Second, Socialism is attractive because it promises free goods and services without having to work for them—that is a powerful incentive to become a Socialist. This promise appeals to the natural greed of man; it ignites the penchant for theft, for dishonesty, and the desire to enjoy life at the expense of others. It appeals to the human desire to find an outlet for envy of those who have more and to shift the blame to someone else for our own failures.

Marx's vision for the world was one where everyone's needs would be met; you would only have to do what you enjoy doing. You would freely choose what you wanted to do. In a text from his 1844 booklet, Marx describes this freedom. After Marxism has remade the world, you would not have to do anything you didn't want to do:

> [This] makes it possible for me to do one thing today and another tomorrow, to hunt in the morning, fish in the afternoon, rear cattle in the evening, criticize after dinner, just as I have a mind, without ever becoming hunter, fisherman, shepherd or critic.[1]

Imagine a world like that!

The goal of Marxism is that no one will *have* to work, or at least no one would have to have a job they dislike. Through a shared economy everyone will have all of their needs met. Who would not want a world in which you could essentially live as you please? The assumption is that others would work to meet your needs, "From each according to his ability, to each according to his needs."[2] Marx never explained how one would distinguish *ability* and define *needs*. Of course, in real life, some people think they need more than others and within time *needs* become *demands* and *demands* will be met with violence.

Economist Joseph Schumpeter described Marx as "an amateur in economics, but a genius in psychology."[3] He looked deeply into the sinful hearts of human beings and appealed to their natural and often base desires. Find a group of frustrated, angry people, and to justify their anger they blame their plight on Capitalism. They are taught that the only reason some people are poor is because some are rich. The reason for the poverty of many other nations is because the United States is rich, and its wealth was created because of "American Imperialism." So, since the wealthy became rich at the expense of others, to accumulate wealth is dehumanizing; it is evil.

In passing, we should note that such reasoning is actually based on what is known as "the zero-sum fallacy," the assumption is that there is only a fixed amount of wealth in the world, so the only way one nation can become richer is if another becomes poorer. Or if you amass a fortune, it is because you trampled on the wealth of others. This of course ignores the fact that wealth can be created by innovation, such as the wise use of resources and the expansion of businesses.[4]

But why not combine democracy with Socialism? Why not blend the two and bring in Socialism through the existing democratic process of America? Make the American dream affordable for everyone!

Welcome to the DSA!

The Democratic Socialists of America

Two important questions must be answered.

Recently a friend asked me a fair question; "What is the difference between Communism and Socialism?" Interestingly, in the *Manifesto*, Marx sometimes uses the term Socialism and Communism interchangeably.

But he also makes this distinction: Once the working class (proletariat) overthrows the ruling class, the communist leaders will emerge out of the working class.

> The communists are on the one hand the most advanced and resolute section of the working class parties of every country, that which pushes forward all others, on the other hand, theoretically they have over the great masses of the proletariat *the advantage of clearly understanding the line of march and the conditions and ultimate general results of the proletariat movement.*[5] (Emphasis added.)

To put it more clearly, once the working class overthrows the ruling class, then out of the masses of the working class there will be elites who will rule; they are the Communists with the greatest wisdom and have a clear understanding of what needs to be done. Socialism (the revolution) is the transformation that brings about the communist ruling class. To summarize, *Socialism is the means, the utopia of Communism is the goal.*

But for our purposes, an even more important question is: Did Marx believe in democracy? The answer is yes. Marx wrote that when the ruling class is destroyed by the proletariat, the revolution is complete, and the Communists are ruling, democracy will have been achieved.[6] So, yes, Marx believed in democracy, namely the triumph of Communism, when class distinctions disappear and the results of the revolution are completed. By *democracy* Marx certainly does not mean free elections whereby the ruling communist government could be ousted. In context, he makes clear that it means that, at last, the masses would be satisfied because they were represented by the Communists in power. There is, of course, a form of democracy in communist countries; after all, they do have elections. But as we know, the opposition is suppressed and sometimes eliminated.

But what about Democratic Socialism in America?

Founded in 1982, the Democratic Socialists of America is a relatively small organization, but it has grown substantially with the emergence of socialist politicians who adhere to its basic premises. They believe that the working people should have a part in regulating the economy and get their "fair share," and that the government should be made to "work for everyone." It would therefore be incumbent on the state to tax the wealthy, regulate businesses, and make living "more affordable." Many of its goals are appealing to all of us.

In contrast to Marxist Socialism/Communism we have described so far in this book, American Democratic Socialists would not say that all private property should be confiscated, although they do speak about implementing laws that control housing and owning some industries. They would not say that religion should be outlawed or that they seek a revolution, envisioning the "forceable destruction of all that exists." But they do speak about *collectivism*; and thus it is important for us to understand the meaning of the word.

Stalin, for example, frequently used the word *collectivism* in his speeches. In this speech from 1933, he said,

> Under the new, collective-farm system the peasants work in common, cooperatively, with the help of modern implements—tractors and agricultural machinery; they work for themselves and their collective farms; they live without capitalists and landlords, without kulaks and speculators; they work with the object of raising their standard of welfare and culture from day to day.[7]

That word *kulaks* refers to wealthy farmers, many of whom were sent to Siberia because their success was in opposition to the equality of the communist cause. In Stalin's Union of Soviet Socialist Republics (USSR), all individual farms had to be consolidated to eliminate the wealthy landowners and to put all agriculture decisions under state control. Stalin said that as farmers worked for the collective, they would eventually benefit. But it was not to be; the state-controlled farms produced less and the state took the grain and sold it to prop up the communist system. Millions starved to death.

In reality, under collectivism, the dignity of the individual had to be erased in favor of the collective—the government expands its control and takes more direct intervention in the lives of its citizens. The individual is unimportant, the ideology is supreme. This must be done to bring about "economic equity." It's called the redistribution of wealth.

So, whenever possible, Democratic Socialists will build a bureaucracy to nationalize businesses, control prices, and grow the size of government to the "benefit" of all the people. To exert such pervasive control, the centralization of greater state power is necessary. Regulations multiply, as taxes are increased. Other more radical changes might be necessary, because once you board a train, it's difficult to exit until it has run all the way to the next station. They align perfectly with Antonio Gramsci's vision of Communism coming "through the long march through the institutions" we described it in chapter 7.

In passing, you have probably noticed that even as socialist politicians blame many of the problems of social order on the rich, they themselves solicit huge sums of money from wealthy capitalists to run their campaigns. They are most happy to take the wealth of capitalists to win elections even though when they win, their policies will eventually cripple those same capitalists and stifle the economy.

They want to tax the rich to distribute the wealth that Capitalism has made, yet they don't realize that without Capitalism there would be less wealth to distribute.

As many have noted, the attraction of Marxism—even of the democratic kind—is that people judge it by its promises, not its results. The promises are emotionally satisfying; we have already listed the promises of free goods and services. What's missing is that this utopian message cannot be applied; it can only exist as a theory. As Thomas Sowell said, "It is hard to imagine a more stupid or more dangerous way of making decisions than by putting those decisions in the hands of people who pay no price for being wrong."[8] Distributing wealth seems like such a great idea but is less appealing when you discover that it is your wealth that is being distributed. Yet, Socialists promise to confront the issues facing their constituency, and this ideal is so compelling that obvious facts will not dampen their enthusiasm for the dream.

Let's notice a number of criticisms of Democratic Socialism.

Socialism Runs Out of Money

Have you noticed that Socialists never talk about *making* money; they only talk about *distributing* it? Imagine that our economy was a pie created by a capitalist economy. Socialists want to cut the pie into various pieces and distribute them more evenly. So, as much as possible, they take control of the economic engines of business to make the government work for everyone. But after the pie pieces are distributed, you are left with an empty pie plate (or near-empty pie plate) with no other pies to distribute. Only the government can bake another "pie," but its restrictions and regulations make it well-nigh impossible. And because there is no personal profit to individuals in baking pies, everything stagnates. It does not abolish *poverty*, but of necessity, abolishes *prosperity*.

Socialism can work for a time until the government runs out of money. Then the state has several options: It can increase taxes and put an unbearable burden on businesses that will cause growth to stagnate; or a country can just print more money, in which case inflation becomes rampant and wages can't keep up with the soaring prices. No wonder people in Russia could only survive if they formed a shadow economy built on bartering outside of the designated channels.

When we were in Russia, we heard one story after another of how the people survived. They paid a repair man with a bag of potatoes and swapped a table for a bed. They traded a day's work in a field for a pair of used shoes. Their ingenuity knew no bounds. We were told that virtually everyone had to have access to vegetables in the fields because they couldn't survive on their wages and pensions, and besides, the stores were empty. So, vegetables were bartered for other goods and services.

Or think of Socialism as a caste system; if you're at the back of the line, you stay there. There can be no easy path forward. Without a profit motive, people will simply not work. Furthermore, businesses need capital to invest and sometimes risk money to obtain new markets, etc. No corporation like Boeing or Apple could ever have developed under a socialistic system. The core software technology that runs our smartphones, especially the popular iPhones and

Android phones, was developed in the United States. While the phones themselves may be made in communist or socialist countries, it is in the capitalist society, primarily in the US, where the core technology developed that makes smartphones work.

Whether it is Russia, China, Cuba, or Albania, the story is the same: When the state owns the means of production, it needs strict wage and price controls; it also needs to restrict the freedom of the people. When we were in Russia in the 1980s, we were told that doctors were not paid much more than other hospital workers, hence there was a shortage of doctors in overcrowded hospitals. Healthcare is rationed, and old people are dispensable. Apparently, it is better that everyone be equally poor than to have some wealthier than others.

You don't have to be an economist to grasp these basic principles.

When the government fixes prices to make them "affordable," the supply of products disappears, and there are shortages; if it makes them higher than the market value, there is an overabundance of supply. If you freeze the cost of rent, owners will be seen as adversaries, and investors will not be investing in the housing market or rental property; if you control the cost of groceries to make them cheaper, gardeners will stop growing vegetables and farmers will not make enough money to harvest their crops. You will end up with stores, such as those in communist counties, with empty shelves, long lines, and continual shortages. Socialism is based on self-defeating dreams.

Under Socialism, failure can never be acknowledged but is met by even tighter government control. Under Capitalism, competition keeps the prices affordable; under Socialism this can only be done artificially by the action of the government, but that action interferes with the ebb and flow of the actual prices a free market allows.

Certainly, the rich should pay their fair share, but to keep shifting the burden onto them restricts their ability to maintain competition and stifles their ability to make new investments that create new capital. Of course, another possibility is to borrow money from future generations. Our cities are already greatly in debt; our individual states are in debt; and as a nation, our national debt is 37-plus trillion dollars! I will not pretend that I understand how we can continue down these paths without an eventual implosion of our economy. Only governments can endlessly keep borrowing (or printing) money; you and I cannot. I believe that at some point, if I might use an illustration from my boyhood, "Someday the sock is going to come unraveled."

Socialism—even of the democratic kind—paves the way for full-blown Communism in this way: Socialism always increases government dependence; people begin to rely on the state for government grants and subsidies of free goods and services. To reverse these policies is nearly impossible. In effect, votes can be bought by the politician promising the most entitlements, which later turn out to be nothing more than empty slogans.

Our Founding Fathers had wisdom we should heed: Thomas Jefferson predicted "future happiness for Americans, if they can prevent the government from wasting the labors of the people under the pretense of taking care of them."[9] And Ben Franklin is quoted as saying, "The people would in time discover they could vote themselves money from the public treasury, which would end the republic."[10]

We can't quote the words of Margaret Thatcher too often: "The problem with socialism is that you eventually run out of other people's money."[11] Yes, it can work for a while, until other people's money dries up. And if we vote ourselves money from the public treasury, yes, that will result in the end of the Republic.

Socialism Does Not Meet People's Needs

I've heard demonstrators shout, "Capitalism is based on *greed*; socialism is based on *need*!" Of course, both systems are often motivated by greed. But there is this difference: Capitalism only works when capitalists create businesses that meet people's needs. Capitalism is dependent on producing a product people will actually want and buy; consumers are voting in favor of Capitalism with their dollars. Therefore, it is based on the obvious principle: If there are no consumers for a specific product, then those products will no longer be made. The power is in the hands of the consumer.

Contrast Socialism, which places the power in the hands of the government elites; it can operate without concern about meeting people's needs. It is in charge of determining what people should have and how much consumers should pay for it. And those in charge of redistributing the wealth can give themselves extra "bonuses" for their hard work. In Socialism, corruption can be conveniently legislated by the state bureaucrats.

A case in point: When we visited Russia in the 1980s, my interpreter told us of a factory that made shoes no one could wear. The contour of the foot within the shoe was wrong and because no one bought them, the shoes were piled high in the warehouse even as the factory continued its production. The workers didn't care that they were making a product no one wanted, because whether the shoes were sold or not, they still received their guaranteed wages from the government. The workers were paid for making what no one could use.

A Romanian friend of mine told me that under Communism, he worked in a foundry where they were required to produce a certain amount of iron products. Much of what they produced was unusable because of bad equipment and shoddy workmanship, but everyone got paid the same: the slackers, the latecomers, and the hard workers all got their guaranteed wages.

Whether it is cars, refrigerators, or public housing, the stories we heard were the same: Nothing worked efficiently, and nothing was made with the customer in mind. The workers did not have to produce anything that satisfied customers. They just had to go to work and produce what the government prescribed.

All Initiative Is Lost

In the communist countries Rebecca and I visited, we noticed a different attitude in the stores. In capitalist countries, store clerks are anxious to please their customers, knowing they are dependent on meeting the needs of their clientele. In a communist/socialist state, the clerks can be dismissive or even rude. They couldn't care less whether you buy their goods because they don't share in the profits; they are locked into their government salaries regardless.

Think of it this way: Suppose a professor in a college would tell his students that at the end of the semester he would average all the grades in the class and each student would receive the same grade, regardless of whether they individually did A+ or D- work. Would that motivate students to work hard and do their best? We can be quite sure that the motivation of the students would largely evaporate.

No one wakes up in the morning excited to work for the state. In Socialism, indifference, laziness, and lack of ingenuity is rewarded with essentially the same wages a hard worker receives. Whether the work is done well or poorly, efficiently or with indifference, all share their poverty equally. Over and over again we heard, "We pretend to work, and they pretend to pay us!"

In the 1950s, Gerald L. K. Smith, warned, "You cannot legislate the poor into freedom by legislating the wealthy out of freedom. . . . The government cannot give to anybody anything that the government does not first take from somebody else."[12] Because the government takes and then gives, it must have tight controls. The more centralized the economy, the more it must rule with an iron fist. And rule with an iron fist, it does.

Which system is more compassionate? The one that, of necessity, has to meet the needs of its customers? Or the economic system that can operate without any benefit to people they claim to serve?

Democratic Socialism Contributes to Corruption

What form of economics is most corrupt? Socialism or Capitalism? Of course, both forms have greed and corruption, a sad but true commentary on the human heart. But both reason and history assure us that Socialism, by its very nature, *spawns* greed and corruption. With Capitalism, the profit motive along with competition keeps the prices down and owners are less likely to tolerate corruption.

In Socialism, you are taught early on that if you want to better your lifestyle it will not be by working harder but by gaming the system. Your job is to find ways to cheat the system to "get what is free," as promised by the government.

As the state of Israel discovered when it began to run its kibbutzim on socialist principles, people began to misuse the system because food and services were "free." They left their lights and heat on longer than necessary because they didn't have to pay market price for electricity. Pets ate at the dining room table because the food was "free." As one of the kibbutzim pioneers said, "It became a paradise for parasites."[13]

A paradise for parasites!

What makes anyone think, "If only the means of production was controlled by the government, the greed would disappear"? Yes, we as humans have self-interests; greed lies deeply in every human heart. But under Socialism, greed is institutionalized due to the incentive to get what is "free." Greed runs amok both among the rulers who distribute the wealth and among the people who try to survive on their "guaranteed income." Under Socialism, you must find creative ways to bypass the government programs to survive.

Of course, Capitalism is far from perfect. Greed, corruption, and vicious competition often abound. And yes, the elites pay themselves large salaries and seek to undercut their competitors. Wall Street has no shortage of loan sharks, huge investors constantly monitoring their profits. But there are strict rules that make prosecution of corruption possible. And since commerce is legally separated from the government, the Department of Justice is expected to prosecute businesses without a direct conflict of interest. Under Socialism the elites who run the government are also those who control the judiciary; therefore, prosecution of corruption is nearly impossible.

Socialism rewards laziness, stifles competition, and restricts individual liberties. Under Socialism, corruption is largely unchecked because it is more difficult to discover and uproot. The bureaucrats who dictate where the money goes are the ones who make the laws and reward themselves. No wonder even the poor under Capitalism fare much better than most of the populace in socialist countries. Venezuelan Daniel Milán notes that "to make a truly socialist country you'd need a bunch of zombies and robots, because real human beings were not meant for socialism."[14] It submerges the individual in an ocean of bureaucracy and tight-fisted regulations.

In the article "Why Socialism Always Fails," John Stonestreet and Timothy D. Padget write,

> Socialism ultimately fails because it is built on flawed anthropology. Socialists claim to be for "the People," but it's always for Humanity and never for humans. According to a socialist vision, the individual receives dignity from society, not the other way around. The individual with his or her unique insight, perspective, and preference becomes an existential threat to the grand socialist project.[15]

Progress down a wrong path is *regress*. Socialism destroys human dignity and teaches that your value is determined by the state, not by the freedom God gives us to display His will and purpose. These words of Winston Churchill are worth repeating: "The inherent vice of capitalism is the unequal sharing of blessings; the inherent virtue of socialism is the equal sharing of misery."[16]

Nevertheless, some people who have grown up in socialist countries will always be enamored with state control. After the fall of the Berlin Wall, a cartoon appeared in a Russian newspaper picturing a fork in the road. One path was labeled "freedom," the other labeled "sausage." As we might guess, the path to freedom had few takers; the path to sausage was crowded with footprints.

There is an expression that is as relevant as yesterday's news. "They are shrinking the forest, but the trees keep voting for the axe, because the axe's handle is made of wood, and the trees think it is one of them."[17]

Clearly, Jesus was not a Socialist. He told a parable about a man who, before he went on a journey, called his servants and entrusted to them his property. "To one he gave five talents, to another two, and to the other one, each according to his ability" (Matt. 25:15). There is no hint that the owner did wrong because each was not given the same amount. The point of the parable was that we are expected to be faithful with what we have been given: "To whom much is given, much is required. (Luke 12:48)."

Of course, we should encourage the initiative to better our position and to make wealth as long as it is done with honesty, legally, and with fairness. Abundance is not inherently sinful as long as it is not prioritized above our spiritual commitment and love for God; there is room in our hearts for only one throne (Matt. 6:24).

To summarize: The more the state owns, the more it controls its citizens; the more it controls its citizens, the more bureaucracy; the more bureaucracy, the more limited our freedoms and initiative to better our place in the world. In the end, those who control the economic system are the ones who benefit from it. As George Orwell put it in *Animal Farm*, the 1945 allegorical satire of the Russian Revolution and Stalin's rise to power: "All animals are equal, but some animals are more equal than others."[18]

The Role of Government

There is plenty of room for disagreement, but surely we all believe that government has an important role in ensuring that standards are met in what is produced and in issuing laws, such as those that keep citizens safe (e.g., border control), that keep them from harming each other, and that protect against corruption.

Let's remember that a number of agencies in America deemed "essential services" are already government run: the postal service, public education, social security, healthcare, Medicare, welfare programs, etc. But what do these government-run programs have in common? None of them make money; the government can only spend money given to it by its citizens. It pays for these services by taking the money of its citizens through taxation. But to increase taxes or to nationalize industries means the source of money would begin to shrink. Democratic Socialism, as discussed above, aims to expand expenditures without a source of creating money except by printing more or raising taxes.

The government should have a safety net for those who genuinely cannot survive without support. The government should be able to prevent monopolies so that no one company can corner the market. Without competition, a business can charge unreasonable prices. But that role is very different than an expansive government program with a "universal guaranteed income."

Meeting the needs of people is best accomplished through private business, ingenuity, and competitive bidding. Without competition there is inefficiency and stagnation. And yes, people game the system.

Let the discussions begin!

The Church, Capitalism, and Money

As Christians, we must step back and ask: What does the above discussion about monetary policy teach us about what money is, *really*? Millions of Christians are surviving under socialist regimes often run by corrupt bureaucrats. Capitalistic countries also have their own share of greed and corruption along with the poor living among the rich. Does all this really matter? A friend of mine gave a lecture on Christian Nationalism and ended by saying, "The great hope for the world is Jesus Christ, not America!"

Who of us would disagree with that? I have devoted my life to preaching the gospel, to sharing Christ with everyone. Of course, Jesus—not the United States—is the great hope for the world. For that, let us be willing to give our lives!

But there is no country in the world that has invested so much wealth in supporting thousands of missionaries to go around the world to tell people that Christ is their great hope than the United States! Capitalism has given many Christians who live in the West the opportunity to make more money than they need. This wealth has fueled missionary projects around the world.

Think of any mission work in so-called developing world countries, and you'll discover almost always they are operated by funds supplied by the West. When mission agencies need funds, they don't look for supporters in socialist countries because they know the Christians there are fortunate if they have enough money to survive. Only a capitalist economy can lift the living standards of ordinary people above subsistence levels.

We need to rethink what money really is and ponder more deeply the teaching of Jesus about how our funds are used. Why did Jesus repeatedly warn about dependence on money? And what did He mean when He spoke about the "true riches"? Why is money so deceitful?

Money makes the same promises as God. In effect money says, "I will be with you in sickness and in health; I will be there when your friends fail you. I will be there when others are starving and there are long lines at food banks. I promise you security, health, and pleasure." Wave big money in the face of most people and they'll lie, cheat, and otherwise throw out their basic principles to get it. The slogan says it: "Get it honestly if you can; get it deceitfully if you must, but *get it*."

Yet money cannot keep its promises. I read a true story about two gold miners who were caught in a terrible blizzard up in the northern woods and were not able to leave in time to escape the coming winter. Months later, they were found starved to death in their hut surrounded by pieces of gold. Money has no inherent value unless it's transmuted into some other form of wealth: food, clothing, or if we are wise, we will invest in eternal riches.

The passage of Scripture about money that lodges most deeply in my heart is what Jesus taught in Luke 16. In essence, the parable He told can be summarized: Use your wealth "so that when it fails they may receive you into the eternal dwellings" (Luke 16:9). In other words, take the money men create and transmute it into a form that will survive inflation, deflation, a change of political regimes, and your own certain death. This, Jesus said, is "the true riches."

All believers—but now I am especially thinking of those who have benefited from Capitalism—will someday stand before the judgment seat of Christ with worthless money left in their banks and retirement funds. When the Lord comes "the heavens will pass away with a roar, and the heavenly bodies will be burned up and dissolved, and the earth and the works that are done on it will be exposed" (2 Peter 3:10). Everything will be canceled. Of that day, we can be certain. As theologian and pastor Francis Schaeffer put it, we must have "capitalism with compassion."[19] Yes, too often Capitalism exploits the poor and appeals to the greed of the human heart. But we must do all we can to make money with the intention of giving it away, transmuting it so that there will be those who will meet us in "eternal dwellings."

Our love and sacrifice should be an attractive alternative to the false hopes of utopian dreams. On our shoulders rests the responsibility of doing what the state might try to do but does poorly: to give our lives to share our wealth to help the needy and build bridges for the sake of the gospel.

To whom much is given, much is required.

CHAPTER 9

What Did Marx Get Wrong and Moody Get Right?

Revolution or Redemption?

With more than just a touch of sarcasm I must ask, "By attempting to destroy belief in God, reducing human beings to disposable material property, destroying freedom and stealing private property, and cruelly punishing those who disagree with the prevailing ideology, what could possibly go wrong?" The answer of course is *just about everything*.

Marx's View of Human Nature

In retrospect, thinkers should have known that Marxism would be a failed system. It is like expecting water to rise above its own source; it is contrary to everything we know about human nature and human reason. It is fundamentally unworkable.

Before there was Marx, there was Robert Owen (1771–1858), one of the forerunners of Communism. He believed that no one was "responsible for his (or her) will and his (or her) own actions because his whole character is formed independently of himself."[1] So, evil exists outside of you, and whatever evil you do is because of forces beyond your control; we are the product of our environment. Marx agreed.

The assumption was that Capitalism makes people greedy, but when it is destroyed, wealth will be created independently of any self-interest. Marx believed that if Communism were implemented, society wouldn't just have a new state, but "a new man." He believed the only reason people committed crimes was because of multiple layers of oppression (the *intersectionality* mentioned earlier); otherwise, people would live in peace, and there would be equality and blessings for all. Having not properly diagnosed the problem, he was destined to find a wrong cure.

Just think about these words from *The Communist Manifesto*: "The Communist revolution is the most radical rupture with traditional property relations; no wonder that its development involves the most radical rupture with traditional ideas. . . . We have seen . . . that the first step in the revolution by the working class, is to raise the proletariat to the position of ruling class, to establish democracy."[2] In the last chapter, we pointed out that democracy for Marx was the result of toppling the present social structure and putting the Communists in charge. The revolution would bring about "democracy," a form of control in which everyone would benefit.

Think of it. Marx and Engels believed that the bourgeoisie were uniformly evil and the proletariat uniformly good. All capitalists were greedy; in contrast, the workers were largely free of self-interest so would rule as Communists, only for the good of others. If the bourgeoisie had all of their property forcibly stolen and the dissenters eliminated, and the working class came to power, this would bring about "justice" and "equity." Those in power would promote the wisdom of a group of elitists (the true Communists) who could be trusted to use their positions not to enrich themselves but would consistently work for the greater good of everyone else. The disparities within human nature would disappear and, yes, utopia would arise. Lenin actually preached that, eventually, there would be no need for government; even the state would vanish, and humans would finally find their stride.

Marx believed that capitalists exploited the poor and manipulated the economic system to suit their own ends; but with incredible naivety, he thought that human nature would suddenly become selfless and caring once a suitable economic environment was provided. Yes, human beings under these conditions would spontaneously act lawfully and, eventually, both the state and the need for laws would wither away.

Keep in mind that the goal of Marxist Socialism is to bring about a strictly communistic society in which a state with the most power is in the control of the fewest elites as possible. After all, they reason, only a few really understand what needs to be done to bring about the utopian dream. These delusions are still believed today.

Apparently, it didn't dawn on Marx and his followers that if one oppressive regime were violently overthrown, it would only be replaced with a regime that would be equally (or even more) oppressive and violent. And with the new class in power taking over the "means of production," these new rulers would greedily take advantage of their new privileges and enrich themselves at the expense of others.

Running a government is no small task. It takes years to organize and grow an economy and maintain order. What made Marx and Lenin think that after the revolution (the "dictatorship of the proletariat"), the masses would gladly hand over their power to be controlled by a few enlightened elites who would know what to do? That they would be able to manage the bureaucracy that is necessary to run a fair and trustworthy government? As it was, the craftiest criminals would rise to positions of leadership, and among them, a dictator would arise.

This blindness to the true nature of man is demonic. Marxists teach people to avoid looking deeply into their own faults but to carefully analyze the faults of others. We could summarize: "Since we evolved through the evolutionary process, the human race did not fall into sin (as Christians suppose), rather, human nature is actually good and getting better; but we still have evil because of various forms of oppression. Since my faults do not originate from within me, I will focus on fixing my outward social and cultural environment by forcing the kind of political and cultural change Marxists insist is needed in our journey to a better world. This is the only salvation we need.

For some people this means that if they can blame sexism, white patriarchy, racism, Capitalism, American Imperialism, and/or some other oppressive influence, they need not deal with their own faults, greed, or failures. To be clear, those evils can and do exist, but they don't excuse our own individual evils and how we ourselves might be contributing to a sinful culture.

Watch some demonstrations against hate and you will see hatred exhibited in speeches and destruction on the streets. We are all guilty; we see the hate of others but not the hate within ourselves. Jesus used the illustration of those who see the speck in other people's eyes but don't see the log that is in their own (Matt. 7:3).

Incredibly, Marx did not understand that if the human race had actually evolved by the process of a random evolutionary cycle, they would have no soul and no God to whom they give an account; then people would cast morality, decency, and compassion aside and revel in the most detestable kind of evil. They could join with the devil in his perverse dreams.

Marx believed in the basic perfectibility of human nature; take away their imposed oppression and everyone will wake every morning excited to go to work even if they derive no benefit from their labors. Since the only reason people do evil is because of external forces of oppression, once the revolution is complete, there will be no need for the police; after all, the police are oppressive and such oppression must be removed. Translated for today: We should defund the police and replace them with social workers.

No wonder Marxism can only exist behind a barbed wire fence patrolled by police dogs and monitored by secret police. It was doomed to ruin what it set out to fix and to exacerbate the inequalities it purported to care about.

Moody's View of Human Nature

Moody saw what Marx did not: Sin resides *in* us and this accounts for the fact that there is oppression *outside* of us. Of course there is systemic evil, but the outside evil reflects the inside evil of the human heart. Moody knew that our biggest problem is ourselves; it is we who live with an inborn sinful desire to use others for our benefit.

Marx thought that if our bodily needs were satisfied, we would live in peace, without envy, without any evil impulses. Moody knew better. He understood the words of Jesus, "Man shall not live by bread alone, but by every word that comes from the mouth of God" (Matt. 4:4). Man has a spiritual need that necessitates he be transformed on the inside, a work only God can do. In other words, people have to be "born again, not of perishable seed but of imperishable, through the living and abiding word of God" (1 Peter 1:23), which lives and abides forever.

Moody preached the biblical doctrine that we are "Ruined by the Fall." He understood that we are, by nature, selfish, driven by a sinful nature and incapable of extricating ourselves from our inborn desire to live our lives at the expense of others. We have an inborn spiritual need that a revolution cannot repair; we don't just need help, we need to be rescued from the depth of our sin by the grace of God. He knew humanity had a problem that humanity could not solve. For that the intervention of God was needed.

As the New Testament so accurately puts it,

> And you were dead in the trespasses and sins in which you once walked, following the course of this world, following the prince of the power of the air, the spirit that is now at work in the sons of disobedience—among whom we all once lived in the passions of our flesh, carrying out the desires of the flesh and the mind, and were by nature children of wrath, like the rest of mankind. *But God . . .*" (Eph. 2:1–4)

What follows in this passage is an exposition of the intervention of God to rescue us from our sins and from ourselves by the grace of God in Christ. That necessitated an inner transformation that no political system can possibly accomplish.

Marx believed he could create a new man by changing his environment; Moody believed that only God could create a new man by changing his heart. "Therefore, if anyone is in Christ, he is a new creation. The old has passed away; behold, the new has come" (2 Cor. 5:17). This gospel of inner transformation has changed millions of lives even when it has not changed their environment. And yes, our present environment is important, but not supremely important. Moody had his priorities right.

Evangelists such as D. L. Moody have often been accused of caring about people's individual spiritual needs to the neglect of their physical needs. Is this a true reading of their lives and record? So, did Moody have a heart to end systemic evil? The answer is yes, and those are some of the lessons we learn as we look into his life in the next section of this book. You will discover that this remarkable man invested all of his energy for the benefit of humanity and the glory of God.

As you read his story ask yourself: How can we explain the connection between his upbringing and his remarkable accomplishments? If you only knew the story of the first sixteen years of his life, the poverty, the death of his father, and lack of education, what would you have predicted his future would be like?

The life of Moody blows away all our false conceptions that a person's background determines their eventual success or failure. His life shows what God does best: Take the most unlikely person and show the world what can happen in a life that is "totally yielded to Him."

Read the story of Moody next, and then we shall return to the graves of Marx and Moody and speak about their legacies, asking ourselves: What will our own legacy be?

PART TWO

D. L. MOODY

DR. GREGG QUIGGLE

Introduction from Gregg Quiggle

Karl Marx is arguably one of the world's most recognizable names. But who is Dwight L. Moody?

If you have read the first part of this book you know how Marx's political and economic philosophy has influenced the world. But the name Dwight L. Moody is lesser known. And yet, during their lifetimes, Moody, not Marx, was on the lips of millions of people in the British Isles and in the United States.

As Dr. Lutzer has noted, I am a church historian by profession. Allow me to start by acknowledging my bias toward Dwight L. Moody. He is one of my heroes. His humility has inspired me. His sincere faith moves me; his passionate concern for the lost, the practical approach to his faith, his quickness to admit mistakes and seek forgiveness, and just the remarkable size of his ministry, especially considering his limitations, are impressive.

However, I am also encouraged to see that he had flaws and made mistakes. Like me, Moody had blind spots and struggles. He was not a plastic saint. Moody himself often noted he was his own biggest enemy.[1] One of Moody's closest colleagues, R. A. Torrey, put it best when he said,

> Mr. Moody was not a faultless man. If he had any flaws in his character, and he had, I presume I was in a position to know them better than almost any other man, because of my very close association with him in the later years of his life; and furthermore, I suppose that in his latter days he opened his heart to me more fully than to anyone else in the world. I think he told me some things that he told no one else. I presume I knew whatever defects there were in his character as well as anybody. But while I recognized such flaws, nevertheless, I know that he was a man who belonged wholly to God.[2]

As we look at Moody's life, I will share a bit about his journey and how he desired to follow the teachings of the Bible as he understood it. At the same time, this should encourage us to reflect on our own lives, learning from Moody's example and allowing Scripture to guide us. Moody shows us what God can do with and through people who give themselves to Him. Moody was a flawed man from a deprived background whom God used mightily.

We'll get to know Moody better by surveying his work so that we can appreciate this often overlooked giant of the nineteenth century.[3] We'll discover that Moody wasn't just concerned about people's souls—though that, of course, was his great passion. We will see how he viewed the issues of his time, particularly the struggles of the urban working class. He saw the same exploitation described by Marx and Engels and did not ignore the needs of the broken, the helpless, and the poor. We might be surprised by his social consciousness and search for practical solutions. We will also consider interpretations of his legacy and the ways in which he has sometimes been misunderstood.

Finally, we will conclude with a brief summary and ideas for application. We will end by going to the graves of Marx and Moody to contemplate their legacy and ask ourselves, what will our own legacy be?

Let's begin.

CHAPTER 1

Introducing Mr. Moody

The Scope of His Legacy

Perhaps the best way to introduce Dwight Moody is with a story from the Sunday school he started in the slums of Chicago. A relatively new Christian, Moody had come to Chicago seeking a fortune. However, his new faith was taking hold, and Moody, himself a poorly educated child of poverty, was burdened by the plight of poor children and had started a Sunday school.

This story, told by a visitor named Reynolds, shows the heart of Dwight Moody.

> The first meeting I ever saw him at was in a little old shanty that had been abandoned by a saloonkeeper. Mr. Moody had got the place to hold a meeting in at night. I went there a little late; and the first thing I saw was a man standing up, with a few tallow candles around him, holding a negro boy, and trying to read to him the story of the Prodigal Son; and a great many of the words he could not make out, and had to skip. I thought, if the Lord can ever use such an instrument as that for His honour and glory, it will astonish me. After that meeting was over Mr. Moody said to me, "Reynolds, I have got only one talent: I have no education, but I love the Lord Jesus Christ,

and I want to do something for Him; and I want you to pray for me."[1]

It is no exaggeration to say that at the end of the nineteenth century Dwight Moody was one of the most recognized men in the English-speaking world. Religion played a major role in public life, and Moody was the "Billy Graham" of his day. In fact, his death in December 1899 was big news in nearly every major English-language newspaper on both sides of the Atlantic.[2]

In the United States, *The New York Times* wrote, "The death of no man now living could so greatly stir the hearts and minds of so great a multitude on both sides of the ocean."[3] A native of New England, Moody was eulogized by Boston's papers. *The Boston Journal* went as far as to compare Moody to Lincoln, writing: "American boys in the next century should study the lives of a model patriot and its preacher of righteousness."[4] Moody's adopted hometown of Chicago added its comments. The *Chicago Daily News* called Moody "the greatest lay preacher and evangelist of this or any other time."[5] On the other side of the Atlantic, *The Manchester Guardian* concluded, "Moody spoke to larger audiences than any man of the nineteenth century."[6] The *Evening News* in London stated that it was impossible "to exaggerate Moody's phenomenal success."[7] Even *The Catholic World* declared, "His prevailing qualities were tireless energy, amazing common sense, unquestioning faith, and human sympathy rarely equaled."[8]

Perhaps the most striking comment was reported in the *Boston Evening Transcr*ipt and is worth repeating. It was made at the funeral service by Rev. H. B. Weston.

> Because D. L. Moody had mastered, or the power of Christ had so mastered, every fibre of his being; because of that completeness of consecration—I hardly dare say it—were Jesus Christ given the same body, the same mental caliber and surroundings, He would fill up his life much as Moody did, and that is the reason to-day that I would rather be Dwight L. Moody in his coffin than any living man on earth.[9]

I would rather be Dwight Moody dead and in his grave, than any man now living. What a testament to Moody's character and influence!

Historians of American religion have often highlighted Moody as a key figure in American Christianity, also noting his influence in the United Kingdom. Most of our readers know of Billy Graham. Next to the Pope, Mr. Graham was the most well-known religious figure from the 1960s until the beginning of this century. He is often referred to as the "father of modern evangelicalism."

If Billy Graham is considered the father of modern evangelicalism, Moody is its grandfather. As one commentator states:

> It was Moody—more than Whitefield, Finney, and Sunday put together—who was Billy Graham's true predecessor. It was Moody whom Graham admired; Moody who, in fact, made it possible for Graham to do what he did. Moody was the architect who drew up the plans and laid the foundation for 20th-century evangelicalism. . . . By the start of the 21st century, the Moody-Graham project had reshaped the skyline of American Christianity and had launched a new kind of ecumenical movement that reached into every corner of the globe.[10]

Graham paid tribute to Moody in some of his final public remarks. Many years after Moody's death, a quote thought to be from Billy Graham started spreading on the internet: "Someday you will read or hear that Billy Graham is dead. Don't you believe a word of it. I shall be more alive than I am now. I will just have changed my address. I will have gone into the presence of God." Actually, the quote paraphrases an original quotation from Moody that appears in the frontispiece of the official biography by his son William, written in 1900. It reads:

> Some day you will read in the papers that D. L. Moody, of East Northfield, is dead. Don't you believe a word of it! At that moment I shall be more alive than I am now. I shall have gone up higher, that is all; out of this old clay tenement into a house that is immortal—a body that death cannot touch; that sin cannot taint; a body fashioned like unto His glorious body.[11]

Graham understood Moody's importance. Writing to one of Moody's relatives, Graham said, "I am wondering if you all are really aware of the many movements that now exist throughout the world that flowed from the ministry of Dwight Moody."[12] Many leading historians agree with Graham's positive view of Moody's influence. Timothy George describes Moody as the "founder of contemporary interdenominational evangelicalism." Michael Hamilton argues that conservative evangelicalism primarily emerged from Dwight Moody's era-defining revivals, missions work, and institution-building. Martin Marty and George Marsden agreed, stating, "The Chicago-based evangelist could plausibly have been called Mr. Revivalist and perhaps even Mr. Protestant"; and "Scarcely a leader in American Protestantism in the next generation, it seemed, had not at some time been influenced by Moody."[13]

Moody was an evangelist. By one estimate, around 100 million people either heard him preach the gospel or read one of his gospel sermons.[14] One speaker at Moody's funeral said he believed Moody reached about 40,000 to 50,000 people each week. J. Wilbur Chapman, a colleague of Moody's, wrote in the year following Moody's death that he "reached more people during his lifetime than any other man possibly in the world's history."[15] He preached not just to crowds but was committed to personally sharing the gospel with at least one person each day.

Moody's Influence in Education

Despite, or perhaps because of, his own modest education, Moody dedicated his energies to founding schools during the latter part of his career. He helped establish five different schools. Some prepared students for college, while others trained Christian workers. All were committed to serving the poor. The five were: the Northfield Seminary for Young Women, Mount Hermon School for Boys, Northfield Bible Training School, Moody Bible Institute, and Glasgow Bible College. Of these, two remain: Moody Bible Institute and the Northfield Mount Hermon School, which resulted from the merger of Northfield Seminary for Young Women and Mount Hermon School for Boys.

Moody also played a key role in shaping the modern Christian publishing industry. Unable to find affordable resources for new believers, he decided to create his own. Working closely with his brother-in-law, Fleming Revell, Moody helped develop collections of books focused on evangelism and discipleship. Many publishers today, including Moody Publishers, proudly trace their roots back to this inspiring initiative.

Moody played a crucial part in establishing modern Protestant foreign missions through his involvement in the Student Volunteer Movement. Some historians and scholars consider this movement the beginning of modern Protestant missions. In fact, it has been described as "history's single most potent mission organization."[16] One missiologist goes as far as to say that the entire movement was indebted to three distinct movements, the most important being Dwight Moody's personal faith. As he put it, the Student Volunteer Movement was a "striking illustration in the simple authenticity of Moody's spiritual life."[17] Moody was a leader in the early days of the Sunday school movement. Sunday schools have played a significant role in shaping both religious and social communities across the United States and the United Kingdom. Especially in cities during the 1800s and early 1900s, these Sunday schools provided not only religious instruction but also education in various subjects. Moody was key in expanding and improving these urban Sunday schools, with his Chicago school serving as an inspiring example.

Concern for the Poor and the Wounded

D.L. Moody was also a trailblazer in urban missions. Although he didn't originate the movement, Moody greatly contributed to the popularization of the YMCA and Rescue Mission efforts. He helped establish the Chicago YMCA and later served as its leader, bringing energetic gospel preaching together with practical support for those in need. Throughout his life, he passionately promoted their work in cities across the United States and the United Kingdom. Their impact on urban communities was truly meaningful during his lifetime and continues to be felt today.

Moody was a pioneer in military ministry. As part of his involvement with the YMCA, he played a key role in founding the US Christian Commission, an organization dedicated to helping troops during the Civil War. This group cared for both Union soldiers on the front lines and Confederate prisoners, providing religious services, counseling, tending to the wounded, and burying those who had passed away. When the Spanish-American War started, Moody kept up his passionate work with the commission, continuing to offer spiritual support to the soldiers.

Moody's work included a wide variety of Christians. He did not work with a single denomination, which was then called "sectarianism." Instead, he worked with many different Protestant groups. Even more remarkably, Moody worked with Roman Catholics. The nineteenth century was a time of open hostility between Protestants and Roman Catholics in both the United States and the United Kingdom. In the United States, prominent Protestant preachers like Lyman Beecher, Horace Bushnell, and later Josiah Strong painted the Roman Church as the "whore of Babylon" and a threat to the American Republic. Multiple newspapers printed anti-Catholic rhetoric. Before the Civil War, at least two Catholic churches and a convent were burned down by Protestant mobs.[18] Given this context, Moody's ability to find support among Roman Catholics for his work was almost astonishing.

Moody believed in the importance of nonsectarianism. As he put it, "If I thought I had one drop of sectarian blood in my constitution, I would open a vein and let it out."[19] The driving impulse behind his nonsectarianism was his burden for evangelism and discipleship. "Oh, yes, let us sink this party feeling and contend for Christ only. Oh, that God may so fill us with His love, and the love of souls, that no thought of minor sectarian parties can come in."[20] While Moody was not anti-denominations, he prioritized evangelism and discipleship over supporting particular denominations.

Moody was an abolitionist. A committed Union supporter, Moody despised slavery. As a young man, he listened to the impassioned abolitionist speeches of William Lloyd Garrison, Elijah P. Lovejoy, and Wendell Phillips. While in Boston, he took part in anti-slavery demonstrations at Faneuil Hall. Moody considered slavery a sin against God. As he expressed it,

> Nations are only collections of individuals, and what is true of the part regarding character is always true regarding the whole. In this country, our forefathers planted slavery and an open Bible together, and didn't we have to reap? Didn't God make this nation weep in the hour of gathering the harvest, when we had to give up our young men, both North and South, to death, and every household almost had an empty chair, and blood, blood, blood, flowed like water for four long years? Ah, our nation sowed, and in tears and groans she had to reap![21]

As a result, he made efforts to promote racial integration in his work. For example, the five schools Moody founded were all integrated. Moody actively recruited students from diverse racial backgrounds. However, Moody's commitment to inclusiveness had its limits. As we'll observe, during his revival efforts in the South, Moody violated his own principles by hosting segregated meetings, with long-term effects.

As one looks back on Moody's life, thousands of ministers and missionaries testify to Moody's personal influence on their lives. Hundreds of rescue missions, orphanages, homes for prostitutes, temperance societies, employment programs, soup kitchens, and other educational initiatives can be traced back to Moody's efforts. Therefore, any attempt to evaluate Moody's work that ignores these facts is simply unfair.

Born in rural New England, Moody's story is the classic American tale: a poor, uneducated boy who lost his father yet eventually became one of the most prominent figures in the English-speaking world. It is a very different story from Karl Marx's. As we shall see, although both felt a responsibility toward the working poor, their views on the origins of poverty and solutions for urban problems could not have been more different.

Moody, Marx, and God

Moody and Marx had incredibly different views about God. As explained earlier in this book, Marx believed that belief in God played a role in maintaining poverty and famously described religion as the "opiate of the masses." He argued that the ruling classes used religion to justify significant economic inequality. Meanwhile, for those in poverty, religion could serve as a comforting escape and false hope—similar to a drug that temporarily dulls their pain.

By comparison, Dwight Moody passionately believed that the gospel of God was the key to overcoming human suffering and offering eternal life. He viewed poverty and misery as stemming from sin, and he believed that only God's grace could truly set people free. Because of this, he saw the Christian faith as the most effective way to help the working poor improve their lives. As we will learn, Moody dedicated himself wholeheartedly to meeting both the spiritual and physical needs of the people during his time.

Unlike Marx, Moody did not attribute all poverty to the exploitation of others; some yes, but not all. He saw other specific causes of urban poverty: alcohol, laziness, and greed. He believed that Christian conversion was the only way to tackle these challenges and encourage a caring attitude toward the poor. In fact, he saw conversion not only as a solution to the underlying problems but also as a helpful way to reduce the effects of urban poverty. Conversion not only addressed individual vices that caused some poverty, but it also transformed everyone into a kind of personal agent addressing poverty. Moody believed every Christian is commanded to serve the poor. Thus, Moody's approach was personal, community-oriented, and practical, grounded in the belief that genuine human change requires God's supernatural intervention. Marx strongly disagreed.

Evangelism and Care for the Poor

As Dr. Lutzer has noted, some historians and others have often unfairly depicted Moody as a man who prioritized evangelism at the expense of social involvement. The most commonly cited evidence for this claim is this quote from Moody:

> When I was at work in the City Relief Society, before the [Chicago] fire, I used to go to a poor sinner with the Bible in one hand and a loaf of bread in the other. Dr. Chalmers used to forbid his missionaries giving away money or supplies. He said those things ought to come by other hands, and I thought he was all wrong. My idea was that I could open a poor man's heart by giving him a load of wood or a ton of coal when the winter was coming on, but I soon found that he wasn't any more interested in the Gospel on that account. Instead of thinking how he could come to Christ, he was thinking how long it would be before he got another load of wood. If I had the Bible in one hand and a loaf in the other, the people always looked first at the loaf, and that was just contrary to the order laid down in the Gospel.[22]

This quote is frequently misunderstood. Moody was talking about putting God first; the sermon text was Matthew 6:33: "Seek first the kingdom of God...and all these things will be added to you." His point was that people should seek God for who He is, not just for material benefits. Moody also explained that evangelists should focus on sharing the gospel, rather than merely distributing money or supplies. He wasn't saying Christians shouldn't help the poor—he was saying that, for evangelists, the main goal should be sharing faith, not just meeting physical needs. Moody wanted people to understand that a relationship with God is more important than simply getting free bread.

In some respects, Moody reflects Jesus' teaching in John 6. Jesus has fed the five thousand and now turns to the crowd and says in verses 26 and 27, "Truly, truly, I say to you, you are seeking me, not because you saw signs, but because you ate your fill of the loaves. Do not work for the food that perishes, but for the food that endures to eternal life, which the Son of Man will give to you. For on him God the Father has set his seal." This leads to an extended teaching where Jesus describes Himself as the "bread of life," and concludes in verse 58 by saying, "This is the bread that came down from heaven, not like the bread the fathers ate, and died. Whoever feeds on this bread will live forever." While Jesus was concerned to support their physical life by providing food, He was even more concerned to provide eternal life.

Moody prioritized evangelism and emphasized preparation for eternal life. His faith was mainly centered on the next life, but he did not ignore present sufferings. His focus on eternity demonstrated a strong commitment to biblical teachings. Moody argued that the Bible reveals the most important aspect of life is one's relationship with God. As Jesus taught, while helping the poor with physical bread, we should also focus on providing the spiritual bread that offers eternal life.

There are multiple collections of Moody's sermons, many of which connect caring for the poor with spreading the gospel. For example, when preaching on Nehemiah, he said: "Reading the Bible and remembering the poor—a combination of faith and works—will always bring joy."[23] An article titled "Hints and Helps, Nuggets from Mr. Moody's Bible" records the following motto, "Do all the good you can to all the people you, in all the ways you can, as long as you can."[24] Together, these words provide a clear and vivid picture of the evangelist. He always valued caring for the poor and never encouraged anyone to forget this important aspect of faith.

As a younger man living in Chicago, he was actively involved in the neighborhoods. He would regularly gather up church leaders and go door to door. Here is how one person described a typical visit. Bounding to the front door, Moody would greet the family with, "You know me: I am Moody; this is Deacon Thane, this is Brother Hitchcock. Are you all well? Do you all come to church and Sunday-School? Have you all the coal you need for the winter?" Moody always asked about their spiritual and physical well-being, in that order, but never one without the other. He made thousands of such visits.[25]

Moody's focus on evangelism was not something new; it reflected the values of early American evangelicals. In the early 1800s, Charles Finney was a prominent evangelist. Much like Moody, Finney prioritized evangelism more than social issues. He did not combine "revival" and "reform" into one initiative; instead, he viewed social reforms—like temperance and ending slavery—as results of genuine spiritual revival conversion.[26]

His evangelical cousins in the United Kingdom also shared his perspective. Among them was Baptist pastor Charles Spurgeon, who beautifully blended evangelical teachings with a strong emphasis on charity for the disadvantaged. He believed that helping those in need naturally flows from genuine faith. Spurgeon often stated that compassion for the poor and needy stems from genuine Christian beliefs, emphasizing the close link between charity and faith in his view of conversion.[27]

Dwight Moody was a dedicated layperson who primarily worked as an evangelist. He often made it clear that he was not a pastor, theologian, or a leader within a denomination. Instead, he was passionate about using his gifts to evangelize and help others, leaving those roles to others. As one biographer noted, Moody's sermon topics were quite limited: "In the region of speculative, historic, or inferential theology, he does not go, not even into the realm of the Church, its institution, orders, and Sacraments."[28] Moody "stayed in his lane" most of the time.

Many people know the saying "Actions speak louder than words," and in Moody's case, this couldn't be truer. At times, Moody's comments on poverty may seem simplistic or even harsh. But what he did demonstrates a deep heart for the poor. His deeds consistently showed his genuine beliefs. Although he was passionately committed to evangelism, he also personally engaged in charitable work, creating opportunities and providing education to support those in need. This shows that when Moody said to give a Bible before bread, he wasn't opposed to Christians helping others in practical ways.

In fact, as leading historian David Bebbington states, "Moody reinforced the existing link between revivalism and social reform. It is unjust to see him as a social conservative. He frequently insisted that there must be a public display of the fruits of the faith, and he was associated with many of the progressive causes of his day." According to a leading Scottish minister, Moody issued a "'Christian call to righteousness and even philanthropy.'" Bebbington concludes, "It is increasingly appreciated that the movement had evangelical roots. Some of them were nurtured in soil prepared by Moody."[29]

Moody's approach to addressing urban social issues had its limits. As we will observe, he sometimes responded in a naive and overly simplified way. As we examine Moody's life, we see that he gradually developed a deeper understanding of the complexity of these issues. However, he didn't quite have a firm understanding of structural or social sin; for him, sin was mainly a personal matter. Many years later, Moody's son, Paul, reflected that nineteenth-century perspectives influenced his father. Most active during the 1870s and 1880s, Moody was regarded as quite progressive for his time, introducing new ideas—even if later standards considered him somewhat outdated.[30]

As we shall see, Moody showed a deep understanding of human struggles, shaped by his upbringing in a single-parent family and his experiences with poverty in rural New England. As a Christian worker in Chicago, he dedicated himself to helping the urban working poor who faced challenges like overcrowding, disease, pollution, tough working conditions, alcoholism, and lack of access to education. Inspired by his biblical studies and personal encounters with hardship, Moody was passionate about evangelism, aiming to meet both spiritual and material needs in poor communities. His faith guided his practical efforts, leading to meaningful changes in many lives and leaving a lasting legacy through ministries that continue to serve those in need. While his views on city life may at times seem naïve, his contributions to social welfare remain significant.

With that context in place, let's turn to Moody's life. This biography is selective, focusing on Moody's background and extraordinary work with the poor, especially those in urban areas. Moody Publishers offers several more detailed books about Dwight L. Moody's life. If you are as interested in Moody as I am, you will find the books listed in the footnote helpful.[31]

CHAPTER 2

Childhood, Poverty, and Conversion

A Child with a Future No One Could Foresee

Unlike Marx, Moody was born into poverty and received only about four years of schooling. He was born in the small town of Northfield, in western Massachusetts. Rural and charming, Northfield had about 1,500 residents when Moody grew up. The village lies along the Connecticut River, less than twelve miles south of the Vermont–New Hampshire border. To this day, Moody's family home sits on a hill with a breathtaking view of the river and the surrounding rolling mountains. The setting truly feels idyllic.

Moody was born to Edwin and Betsy Moody on February 5, 1837, his mother's birthday. He was the seventh of nine children. Despite their love for each other, the Moody household faced hardships. The family was poor, and Edwin reportedly struggled with alcohol. These challenges made for a tough future for Dwight, especially since their situation worsened when he was just four years old.

In 1841, Edwin, a bricklayer, returned home early, complaining of pain; he died that evening. Betsy, eight months pregnant with twins and with seven other children under age thirteen, faced hardship as Edwin's debts led debt collectors to seize household items. She asked the children to hide the cow in the trees, knowing that the debt collectors would have confiscated her too. Edwin's death was a devastating blow to young Dwight Moody, his siblings, and, of course, his dear mother. Young Moody's early years were defined by poverty and scarce opportunities.

The death of his father would influence Moody for the rest of his life. Reflecting on it later in a sermon, he said, "The first thing I remember was the death of my father. It was a beautiful day in June when he fell suddenly dead. The shock made such an impression on me, young as I was, that I shall never forget it. I remember nothing about the funeral, but his death has made a lasting impression upon me."[1] As an adult, Moody often exhibited signs of the loss's impact. Most notably, he struggled with anger and conflict avoidance, symptoms commonly linked to this type of trauma.

Betsy, devastated and nearly broke, faced the immediate task of caring for her family. Several trusted friends advised her to split up the family to make ends meet, but she was determined to keep everyone together. With her brothers' help, she succeeded. The family also received support from a local church, despite their limited involvement in organized religion. One local church showed Moody a kind of faith that was practical and loving.

Specifically, the local Unitarian minister, Oliver Everett, quickly became friends with the family during their difficult time. Everett was young and had recently graduated from Harvard. Northfield was his first pastorate. It's worth noting that Everett and the church's "Unitarianism" seem somewhat confusing. The entire family was baptized in the church "in the name of the Father and of the Son and of the Holy Ghost." Some even claimed that Everett was, in fact, an orthodox Christian. Unitarianism was more flexible and less strictly non-Trinitarian than it became later in the nineteenth century, and Everett reflected that flexibility.[2]

An early biographer of Moody describes Everett as a faithful friend to Betsy and all her children.

> He would visit them betimes, cheer them up with some pleasant words, settle quarrels among the boys, give the little ones a bright piece of silver all around, and bid the mother to keep on praying; telling her God would never forget her labor of love. One time he took little Dwight into his family to do errands and go to school—a work of charity, which by all accounts must have sorely tried his patience. The good man was often perplexed what to do with the boy, being forced to laugh at his pranks in spite of himself, when he felt his duty to be stern and severe.[3]

Everett supported Betsy's desire to keep the family together telling her, "Not to part with the children but keep them together as best she could, to trust God and to bring them up for him."[4]

In response, Mrs. Moody and her family joined the church and were consistent attenders. Later in his life, Moody would testify to the strong influence the young minister had on him as a boy. In fact, Moody became a recruiter for Everett. As one biographer explains, Moody "and his brother George frequently acted as aggressive home missionaries in securing recruits for the village Sunday-school."[5]

Although Moody attended Sunday school, he found sermons boring and disliked listening to them. His admiration for Everett was rooted more in Everett's compassion than in his sermons. Everett showed genuine care for Moody and his family, making a deep impression. Moody recalled Everett's kindness and saw in him a reflection of a loving God who cares for widows and orphans. This theme of God's love became a central part of Moody's later work.

However, the Unitarian Church was just one part of Moody's journey in faith. After Edwin's death, Moody's mother played a significant role. Before his death, Edwin had given Betsy a Bible. One of Dwight's siblings recounted how this Bible and prayer became significant in her life, recalling how she was often heard weeping and praying over the Bible. Later, the child would look at the Bible and found her mother had marked Jeremiah 49:11, "Leave thy fatherless children, I will preserve them alive, and let thy widows trust in me."[6] Betsy found strength in this Scripture and taught her children to pray, trusting that God would care for orphans and widows. Dwight recalled moments when Betsy was overwhelmed by her children, saying she would retreat to her room to pray for wisdom and patience, asking God for help to maintain order. At her funeral, Moody also remembered waking up to hear his mother praying aloud, pouring out her burdens to God.[7]

While there's not a lot of detailed information about Betsy Moody's specific early Christian beliefs, we do know she regularly led family devotions and kept a sincere prayer life. Moody's sons, Paul and William, recall that Dwight mentioned that Mrs. Moody would read to her children in the evenings from a large family Bible or a book of devotions.

There are also references to morning prayers and devotional readings.[8]

While Betsy worked hard to keep them together despite facing tough financial challenges, she frequently had to send the boys to stay with other families during the winter months. For Dwight, this arrangement lasted seven years after his father's passing. During that time, schooling became a luxury. His education was limited to approximately four years, from ages six to ten, at the local school. Not only was Moody's formal education constrained by his limited time in the classroom, but his personality likely also shaped his educational experience.

Specifically, Moody was a restless, high-energy person, not much given to study. He grew into a strong man, filled with what seemed like endless energy. Years later, Moody would preach for weeks without much rest between meetings.

This description of his preaching demonstrates his high level of energy. "Moody seemed to seize the idea that his messages were to be delivered over wires kept hot and that there was neither time nor money to be wasted in their delivery."[9] The observer continued noting in passages of intense excitement the sentences possessed an explosive quality "suggesting a pack of fire crackers set off by accident."[10] Another described that his sermons' endings had the feel of a cavalry charge, saying one either went with it or got out of the way.[11] The speed of his delivery combined with his limited vocabulary meant he rarely used words with three or four syllables. For example, some claimed Moody "was the only man living who could say Jerusalem in two syllables."[12]

Based on the description of Moody as an adult, it's no surprise that his childhood portrait is just as lively. Dwight was energetic, rambunctious, and a little mischievous. Though mostly harmless, he earned a reputation at school and in the local community for various pranks. These included incidents such as water-filled bathtubs, staged town temperance meetings, and cats disrupting school Shakespeare performances, among others. It seems unlikely that Moody was diligent in his studies during the limited years he spent in school.

> The lack of education was apparent in his early adulthood. His uncle said that when Dwight tried to read the Bible aloud, it was almost impossible to understand him. He skipped entire words because he did not know them or how to pronounce them.[13]

Other evidence comes from some of his correspondence as a young man. Here is an unedited excerpt from a letter written to his brother when Moody was twenty—yes, twenty!— and shows that his education was very limited:

> I think we have things sometimes come a bo(?) us to try ower faith and God likes us to cling on as the Samest sais in one place God likes to chastise them whome he loves so let us pray for each other. I have brout you befor God in my prayers & hope you have done the same.14

His Conversion

Driven and ambitious, Dwight quickly grew bored with Northfield by age seventeen. As a result, Moody moved to Boston, hoping to gain wealth. When job opportunities were limited, he worked for his uncle, Samuel Holton, at Holton's shoe store. Uncle Samuel made it a condition of employment that Moody attend Sunday school at Mount Vernon Congregational Church in Boston. During his time there, Moody caught the attention of a middle-aged teacher named Edwin Kimball. Concerned about Moody's spiritual health, Kimball visited Holton's store to discuss Moody's soul.

As Kimball described it, he decided to visit Moody and "speak to him about Christ and about his soul." He said, "I found Moody" and "I went up to him at once . . . I simply told him of Christ's love for him. . . . It seemed the young man was just ready for the light that then broke upon him, and there, in the back of that store in Boston, he gave himself and his life to Christ."[15]

It's unclear how much of the gospel Moody truly understood. Soon after, he tried to become a full-fledged member of the Congregational church where Kimball taught Sunday school. As part of the process in the Congregational denomination, people were required to be interviewed by the leaders of the church and give a clear testimony. This, however, was a problem for Moody, and he was initially denied membership. The reports from his meeting with the church leadership are revealing. When asked, "Mr. Moody, what has Christ done for us all—for you—which entitles Him to our love?," his reply was, "I don't know, I think Christ has done a good deal for us; but I don't think of anything in particular as I know of."[16] After the interview, the church records state,

> Dwight L. Moody. Boards 43 Court St. Has been baptized. First awakened on the 21st of April. Became anxious about himself . . . saw himself a sinner, and sin now seems hateful and holiness desirable. Thinks he has repented. Has proposed

> to give up sin and feels dependent on Christ for forgiveness . . . loves the Scriptures . . . prays once a day . . . and desires to be useful . . . religiously educated . . . been in the city a year from Northfield in this state. Is not ashamed to be known as a Christian. 18 years old.[17]

Moody reapplied and was interviewed again several months later. Although his testimony improved, it remained hardly impressive. However, this time, he was admitted. What convinced the committee was his earnestness, not his understanding of doctrine.[18] That same earnestness would become a hallmark of his later preaching.

Despite the confusion in his testimony, Moody had changed. Later, he would describe it as follows: "Before my conversion, I worked *towards* the Cross, but since then I have worked *from* the Cross; then I worked to be saved, now I work because I am saved."[19] This event played a crucial role in shaping Moody's perspective on the huge challenges faced by the industrializing Western world. In a very real way, it inspired a heartfelt commitment to serve the last, the least, and the lost.

Looking back on these years, Kimball commented,

> I have seen few persons whose minds were spiritually darker than was his when he came into my Sunday School class; and I think that the committee of the Mount Vernon Church seldom met an applicant for membership more unlikely ever to become a Christian of clear and decided views of Gospel truth, still less to fill any extended sphere of public usefulness.[20]

As the rest of his life would prove, their initial impression would turn out to be stunningly wrong.

CHAPTER 3

A Man in a Hurry

"Chicago, Here I Come!"

Moody described himself as "a man of impulse." He said, "Almost everything I ever did in my life that was a success was done on impulse."[1] By 1856, Moody was tired of Boston and headed west to the thriving city on the Midwestern plains, Chicago. His goal was to make money selling shoes, and yes, he did very well. Yet he never lost his burden for the plight of poor children. Soon after his arrival, Moody established an independent Sunday school in one of the city's most impoverished neighborhoods.

The school's first location was in a section of the city known as "Little Hell," housed in an abandoned saloon. Descriptions from the *Chicago Tribune* in 1875 offer a glimpse of the neighborhood. The district was inhabited by a small "German element. There are Irish, Bohemians, Poles, and Scandinavians. All these are of the poorest and most wretched class. They are the Communists who would like nothing better than to incite an open riot." The newspaper states that the area was "overflowing with juveniles—ragged, hatless, saucy, dirty" and playing "in little groups along the gutters." The difference between boys and girls was almost imperceptible except for "a slight difference in dress." The narrow streets were clogged with "small boys, geese, and hogs. One little chap, with only half a pair of trousers (one leg being quite bare)," stated that his father didn't do anything for a living. Another child of about eight said "his father and mother were both in jail. The manifest arrogance of his tone was no less amusing than the deference paid to him on that account by his companions." The writer concludes:

> But space cannot be given to further details of the interesting characteristics of this neighborhood. Much might be said of the winding alleys, lined with tumble-down little sheds, each of which is thickly populated with human beings. Squalor and filth reign here supreme. Shock-headed children with dirt-begrimed faces peer desolately out of hat-stuffed windows. Sometimes pale women may be seen inside, bending toilsomely over the needlework. Yes oftener, the faces that stare and glare from these hovels are bloated and blear-eyed, telling the monotonous story of wasted lives—over-powered, stupefied, and brutalized by the hideous monster. Intemperance. There is room for missionary effort in "Little Hell."[2]

These were Moody's students, poor Irish, Scandinavian, and German immigrant children. Moody understood these poor children; he knew their plight. Moody connected with the uneducated and rambunctious children, and they responded to him. A friend from these early days described Moody as having an "intense and almost womanly love for children. He never seemed happier than when in the midst of a crowd of boys and girls, with whom he romped in the wildest fashion."[3] Moody not only taught these children but also provided them with food and clothing. On another occasion, one of his students, a young boy, summed up best his experience at Moody's Sunday school. The boy's family had moved to a different part of the city, a very long walk from the school. When asked why he kept attending, he simply replied, "They love a fellow over there."[4]

It was also dangerous work. Moody often faced alcoholic fathers, risking his own physical safety. One biographer recounts a story of Moody entering a home with several children and finding their father's whiskey jug; he poured it out in the street. When he returned the next week, the father confronted him and threatened to beat him. Moody replied, "I emptied the jug for the good of yourself and your family. If I am to be thrashed for it, let me pray for you all before you do it." Falling to his knees, he prayed sincerely for the family. By the time he finished, the father had calmed down and allowed the children to attend his Sunday school.[5]

An early colleague also tells of Moody visiting Roman Catholic families in the slums "and sometimes narrowly [escaping] with a whole head." One enraged father was "exceedingly mad at Moody for coaxing his young papists away"; others "on seeing his beaming face and sturdy form coming upstairs, or in at the door, would sometimes seize a club, and rush at him with oaths and curses." At such times, he used to say, his legs were his best friends.[6]

However, Moody gained favor among the children and gradually earned acceptance from their parents, becoming their de facto minister. In fact, some of the Irish boys started calling him, "Father Moody."[7] Later, Moody would say, "When sickness and death came into their families, they used to send for me. When the ministers were away, I was frequently sent for from other parts of the city."[8]

During these years, Moody frequently led or attended three to four funerals daily. He recounted the story of a four-year-old girl from his Sunday school who had passed away. When he received the news, he visited the family, finding the mother devastated and the father intoxicated. The family depended on the mother's income from laundry work. They were broke and unable to afford a coffin or a marker. Moody covered the costs for both. Afterward, he remarked, "I will never bury a child again in a pauper's grave as long as I live."[9] He kept his word; unknown numbers of poor children were given decent burials by Moody.

Welcoming the President

The school expanded quickly and gained a reputation that reached beyond Chicago. Even the president-elect, Abraham Lincoln, learned about the Sunday school and made a brief visit in November 1860. Although Lincoln intended only to observe, Moody insisted that Lincoln speak to the children. Lincoln agreed, saying, "I was once as poor as any boy in this school, but I am now President of the United States, and if you pay attention to what is taught here, some of you may yet become President of the United States."[10]

As the Sunday school grew, Moody struggled with his own sense of calling. Moody had come to Chicago in search of wealth, but he increasingly felt drawn to ministry. The key event in his struggle involved a girls' class at the Sunday school. There was one particular class of girls who were especially difficult. Moody had assigned one teacher to work with them, but the teacher eventually fell ill with a terminal disease. He came to Moody and explained he needed to leave the school as he was returning home for his final days. He told Moody he was deeply grieved that none of his students were Christians. After listening to the man, Moody agreed to go with him to visit each girl individually. In his biography, Lyle Dorsett describes what happened:

> Over the next ten days as the teacher found his strength, Moody helped him make calls on the other girls. Several days later the teacher came to Moody with good news—the last girl had yielded her heart to Christ. "I'm going home tomorrow. I have come to bid you good-bye." Moody asked him to come to one last meeting of the class that night. The weak but joyous teacher agreed to a farewell time of prayer.[11]

Moody described the final prayer meeting as follows, saying the teacher,

> prayed for me as superintendent of the school; after he prayed I prayed; and when I was about to rise, to my surprise one of those scholars began to pray, and she, too, prayed for the superintendent. Before we rose from our knees every one had prayed. It seemed as if heaven and earth came together in that room. The next day I went back to the store, but, to my great amazement, I had lost all ambition for business.[12]

From this point on, there would be no confusion or struggle for Moody about his life's call; the desire for business success was gone.

As Moody's involvement with the Sunday school expanded, he also became active with the Chicago YMCA. In

1860, now committed to full-time Christian ministry, he left his business career to join the YMCA as its first full-time employee, serving as the city missionary. In this position, Moody dedicated himself to aiding the poor. The annual report from 1861–1862 described Moody as giving "his entire time and energies in executing the several plans of doing good [charitable distributions of donated food, fuel, and clothing] referred to herein."[13]

It is clearly unfair to say Moody cared only for people's souls, not their bodies or living conditions. Writing home in 1862 Moody explained:

> I am very sorry I have not answered you 3 last letters but I have so much to do I could not find time. . . . I take care of the poore of the city. I have some 500 or 800 people that are dependent on me for their daily food & new ones coming all of the time. I keep a sadall horse to ride around with to hunt up the poore people with & then keepe a nother horse & man to carry around the things with & then I have a man to waite on the folks as they come to my office. I make my headquarters at the rooms of the Young Mens Christian Association & [I have three meetings to attend each day] besides calling on the sick & that is not all [I] have to go into the countrey about every week to buy wood and provisions for the poore also coal wheet meal & corn then I have to go to hold meetings.[14]

The pattern continued in 1867 when YMCA distributed $24,325.38 worth of bread, clothing, and coal (about $550,000 in 2025 dollars). More than 3,800 families, including 2,300 immigrants, received aid.[15] During these years, Moody led a simple life. He moved around, with one biographer writing,

"He lived on benches in various hideaways, eventually taking a small room in a makeshift YMCA facility where he did some janitorial work and slept on chairs lined up under the staircase."[16] An early benefactor, John Farwell, also noted that Moody was giving away a portion of his savings from his earlier work to help the poor.[17] In fact, the treasurer for the YMCA recalled, "Mr. Moody was fertile in schemes and expedients for raising money for the Lord's work; but of the many tens of thousands of dollars which he secured for the Association, he received nothing whatever for himself."[18]

Moody also changed the social structure of the Chicago YMCA. He believed the wealthy and educated had an obligation before the Lord to serve those less fortunate. As one biographer put it, Moody brought the "cultured and the wealthy to the assistance of the ignorant and the poor."[19]

Thank God for Emma

Around this time, he also met Emma Revell, an educated woman born in London in 1843. She immigrated with her parents at age six. Reflective and calm, she balanced his impulsiveness and worked to improve his education. Under her guidance, his writing and spelling improved. They married in 1862. Emma was crucial to Moody's ministry, and he often admitted he wished he had asked her for advice more often before making decisions.

By 1866, he had advanced through the ranks of the YMCA to become its president. Under his leadership, the YMCA greatly expanded its efforts among Chicago's working class.[20] It was also through his engagement with the YMCA that Moody encountered the American Civil War.

As the war progressed, the YMCAs in the Northern states banded together to form the United States Christian Commission. The Christian Commission served the physical and spiritual needs of both Union and Confederate troops.[21] Moody was the first delegate sent out by the Commission. Initially, he was assigned to serve Union forces under General Ulysses S. Grant in Kentucky. By the end of the conflict, he had traveled to the front nine times to minister to the troops. In addition to his tours to the front, Moody ministered to Southern prisoners at Camp Douglas, a prisoner-of-war camp located just south of Chicago.[22]

Seeing the Dead and Wounded

Specifically, Moody was with the wounded after the battles of Pittsburg Landing, Shiloh, and Murfreesboro. Moody was also at Chattanooga and among the first to enter Richmond at the end of the war.[23] The Civil War was a terrible and bloody conflict. Moody experienced it firsthand. Shiloh was especially brutal. The final number of dead or missing was 13,000 on the Union side and 10,500 on the Confederate side. The total casualty counts of 23,500 exceeded the combined American casualties of the American Revolution, the War of 1812, and the Mexican-American War.[24]

This brief description of the aftermath of the battle provides a sense of the horror:

> That night the dead lay everywhere. Neither army had developed a system for gathering the dead. General Grant said, "a person can walk in any given direction without stepping on

ground." In a Confederate camp that night, one soldier said, "You can hear the screams of the injured. They screamed for water, God heard them for the heavens opened and the rain fell." Flashes of lightening showed vultures feeding on the ungathered dead.[25]

Moody would later say, "I could hear the groans of dying men, and I helped bear away some of the wounded, and I saw the scene in all its terrible reality."[26]

When not at the front, as part of his Christian Commission work, Moody was involved in forming an employment service for wounded soldiers. In 1865, the bureau found work for 1,435 men, 124 boys, and 718 girls. Between 1867 and 1868, it secured another 3,411 jobs, and it found employment for nearly 9,000 people from 1869 to 1871. In addition, the bureau provided temporary employment for scores of others.[27]

During these years, Moody's focus was not solely on the US Christian Commission. The Sunday school continued to expand, often drawing over 1,000 children and 300 of their parents on a typical Sunday. Moody had no intention of founding a church; he consistently urged the families of new converts to join Bible-teaching churches. The Sunday school was created because Chicago's existing churches couldn't reach the impoverished in the slums. Previously, Moody had attempted to bring boys to church, but it failed; the boys were unruly and loud, and he was politely asked to take them elsewhere. Even after conversion, these children and their families often felt out of place in existing churches.[28]

The Moody Church of Chicago

Moody, disappointed that his children and their families felt unwelcome in established churches, attempted to organize several pastors to form a "union church," but the effort failed. As a result, he decided to establish an independent church. This approach aligned with his strong nonsectarian principles. Consequently, the Illinois Street Church was founded in 1864.[29]

The church was situated in the middle of Chicago's impoverished North Side, at the corner of Illinois and Wells Street. The design was simple—so simple that one observer remarked, "It looks as if pains had been taken to make it as plain as possible so that no one, however poor, might be driven away by any outward display."[30]

The signage reinforced the architecture. Signs read, "Ever welcome to the house of God are strangers and the poor," and "The seats are free." The latter might seem strange to the modern reader, but the practice in those days was to "rent" or "purchase" pews. This was a way to support the church, but it also led to social segregation, making it hard for the poor to attend. But Moody refused to accept that; in his view, no poor person should ever be turned away from a church—this is exactly where they should come for help!

Although he was never officially the pastor, Moody played a vital role in the congregation's life, often speaking there and advising its leadership. The church consistently helped the poor. This was especially clear after the Great Chicago Fire of 1871. Although its building was destroyed, the church quickly set up a temporary structure and immediately offered aid to those affected by the fire.

Over time, the church grew and relocated to another site, and when that building proved to be too small to hold the crowds, it relocated a mile farther north to LaSalle and North Avenue, where it is today. This beautiful structure was built in a short span of thirteen months and dedicated in November 1925. Only then was it officially renamed The Moody Church. Eventually, it became one of the leading evangelical churches in the nation and still ministers to the spiritual and social needs of downtown Chicago. Dr. Lutzer, who wrote the first section of this book on Karl Marx, was the senior pastor there for thirty-six years.

By the end of the Civil War, Moody was increasingly in demand as a speaker. However, the stress of his lifestyle began to catch up with him. The strain of running the YMCA, the Sunday school, starting the Illinois Street Church, dealing with the horrors of Civil War battlefields, and maintaining his role as husband proved too much for him.[31] Thus, in 1867, on a doctor's advice, Moody and his wife, Emma, headed for England for a break from ministry.[32]

CHAPTER 4

Learning from His Brethren in the United Kingdom

Cooperation, Expansion, and Evangelism

Moody's trip to England was crucial in shaping his future ministries. One example was his experience with George Mueller and his work with children. Mueller was already well known for his efforts with orphans in the English city of Bristol. Like Moody, he felt a strong burden for poor children. In Mueller, Moody found a kindred spirit. After going to Bristol to examine Mueller's work, he described the visit in a letter to his mother: "The great orphan schools of George Mueller are at Bristol. He has 1,150 children in his house, but never asks a man for a cent to support them. He calls on God, and God sends money to him. It is wonderful to see what God can do with a man of prayer."[1] One biographer noted that after Moody's time at Bristol, he concluded that the same work could be done back home: "If God could help Mueller feed, clothe, and house thousands of England's street urchins, Moody believed He could certainly help ease the burdens of the hundreds of bruised and broken unfortunates of Chicago."[2]

He also met William Pennefather. Pennefather was an Irish Anglican who organized the Mildmay Conference, an annual gathering of Christian workers. One of the ministries at the conference was an order of deaconesses created by Pennefather. The goal was to train women to work among the urban poor. They were to lead Bible studies and provide medical and practical care. The combination of practical care, spiritual care, and biblical training would later influence the ministry goals of some of Moody's schools.

Moody's most meaningful connection was with Charles Spurgeon. He had admired Spurgeon even before he set foot in England. As soon as Moody arrived, he eagerly went to Spurgeon's church. Of attending his first service, Moody later wrote, "When Spurgeon walked down to the platform, my eyes feasted upon him, and my heart's desire for years was at last accomplished."[3] Moody followed Spurgeon for several more days, listening to Spurgeon speak during a series of special meetings at the Agricultural Hall.[4] Moody won Spurgeon's attention, and the two spent four days together, which was quite impressive considering Spurgeon's busy schedule. At the end of the trip, Moody professed, "He sent me back to America a better man."[5]

This would be the beginning of a long relationship. Speaking at Spurgeon's church in 1884, Moody noted, "I have been here a great many times since [1867], and I never come into the building without getting a blessing to my soul."[6] One historian concluded that Moody "studied at Spurgeon's feet whenever he visited Britain."[7] One indication of the depth of their relationship comes after Spurgeon's death. Spurgeon's wife, Susie, had a copy of Spurgeon's personal pulpit Bible sent to Moody with the following inscription:

> Mr. D. L. Moody, from Mrs. C. H. Spurgeon. In tender memory of the beloved one gone home to God. This Bible has been used by my beloved husband, and is now given with unfeigned pleasure to one in whose hands its service will be continued and extended.
> S. Spurgeon. Westwood, London, Nov. 20, 1892.[8]

After receiving this Bible and a complete set of his sermons, Moody eagerly looked to Spurgeon's writings for guidance on any part of the Bible he was interested in studying.[9] Given their relationship, it is worth briefly examining Spurgeon's social views.

This recent scholar's description effectively captures his work.

> Spurgeon is partly remembered for opposing the downgrading of orthodox theology. He is partly remembered for standing against higher critical German scholarship—a movement that swept across the English Channel and created a crisis of faith in English pews. But Spurgeon's more lasting legacy—his more permanent contribution—is found instead in the children he proactively rescued with his orphanages, in the lives that were changed through an untiring uplifting of Christ, in the aggressive marketing and distribution of his sermons, in the funneling of his own funds to support sixty-six social ministries to balm London's wounded and marginalized population. Spurgeon threw more of his weight into preaching the gospel rather than defending it.[10]

The sixty-six ministries mentioned above included, but were not limited to, "a pastor's training college, two orphanages, a ministry to needy widows, a clothing bank, a ministry to policemen, an outreach to prostitutes, a ministry to the blind and a host of children's ministries."[11]

As one scholar concludes,

> Spurgeon proactively sought to provide aid and relief for orphans and widows, for the sick and infirm and for the extreme poor of London. He advocated for London's lower classes, for the uneducated and the illiterate and even for slaves in the American South. Spurgeon believed each individual Christian was called to engage in works of benevolence and to minister to the most vulnerable.[12]

However, Spurgeon was not a Socialist. In his preaching in the late 1880s and early 1890s, he made this clear. Remember, his ministry coincided in London with Karl Marx and Frederich Engels; already then, Socialism was gaining some adherents. Spurgeon exclaimed, "I would not have you exchange the gold of individual Christianity for the base metal of Christian socialism." Later, he would reiterate his beliefs: "Great schemes of socialism have been tried and found wanting; let us look to regeneration by the Son of God, and we shall not look in vain."[13]

Spurgeon was passionate about the idea that individual salvation was the essential solution. He believed that overcoming vices would liberate people, empowering them to help others through charity. His dedicated efforts to fight poverty in London showcase his commitment and beliefs. As Spurgeon explained it, "To me, a follower of Jesus means a friend of man. A Christian is a philanthropist by profession, and generous by force of grace; wide as the reign of sorrow is the stretch of his love, and where he cannot help, he pities still."[14]

Spurgeon's beliefs closely reflected Moody's, strengthening Moody's approach and inspiring him to follow Spurgeon as a model. Spurgeon's influence can be heard in this 1890 quote from Moody: "We have too much wealth and too much poverty. Why don't some of the people who have made their fortunes stop and go out into the highways and byways and help the poor? That's my idea of socialism, and it's founded on the ideas of Christ."[15]

Feeling energized and inspired by his new friends, Moody came back from his 1867 trip to the United Kingdom full of fresh enthusiasm and quickly got back to his challenging work schedule. Slowing down was not part of Moody's DNA. However, Moody's ministry in Chicago would take a dramatic turn because of one of the greatest urban tragedies in American history: the Chicago fire of 1871.[16] The fire had a devastating effect on Moody. He and his family escaped personal harm, but their home was destroyed. His ministries suffered as well. The YMCA and the Sunday school were both destroyed.[17]

As a result, Moody threw himself into fundraising. He traveled to the East Coast to raise the funds needed to rebuild the ministries.[18] This was a challenging period; Moody grew tired of asking for funds and began to wrestle internally again with his sense of calling. His conflict reached its peak during a second profound religious experience in New York in 1871. Here is how he described it.

> "My heart was not in the work of begging," he said. "I could not appeal. I was crying all the time that God would fill me with His Spirit. Well, one day, in the city of New York—oh, what a day!—I cannot describe it, I seldom refer to it; it is almost too sacred an experience to name. Paul had an experience of which he never spoke for fourteen years. I can only say that God revealed Himself to me, and I had such an experience of His love that I had to ask Him to stay His hand. I went to preaching again. The sermons were not different; I did not present any new truths, and yet hundreds were converted. I would not now be placed back where I was before that blessed experience if you should give me all the world—it would be as the small dust of the balance."[19]

The impact of these two significant events—the fire and his encounter with the Holy Ghost—truly transformed Moody's life. From this point on, Moody enthusiastically embraced his new calling as a traveling evangelist, focusing his energy on reaching out to urban communities.[20]

Transatlantic Evangelist and Christian Leader

Moody would launch his itinerant career with a trip to the British Isles and Ireland. During a stop in Dublin in 1873, Moody would meet the British Evangelist Henry Varley. Varley would utter a challenge to Moody that marked another turning point in Moody's career. At the meeting, Varley said to Moody, "The world has yet to see what God will do with and for and through and in and by the man who is fully and wholly consecrated to Him." Dwight Moody heard those words. Later, he would say to Varley,

> Those were the words sent to my soul, through you, from the Living God. As I crossed the wide Atlantic, the boards of the deck of the vessel were engraved with them, and when I reached Chicago, the very paving stones seemed marked with "Moody, the world has yet to see what God will do with a man fully consecrated to him." Under the power of those words, I have come back to England, and I felt that I must not let more time pass until I let you know how God had used your words to my inmost soul.[21]

If the trajectory of Moody's life was changed by the words of Edwin Kimball, Varley's challenge would become his marching orders. One of Moody's closest associates, R. A. Torrey, recounts a conversation with Moody who had once told him, "Torrey, if I believed that God wanted me to jump out of that window, I would jump." Torrey commented later, "I believe he would. If he thought God wanted him to do anything, he would do it. He belonged wholly, unreservedly, unqualifiedly, entirely, to God."[22]

When Moody did return to England driven by Varley's comments, he had evolved as an evangelist. Specifically, he had teamed up with a singer. Although tone-deaf himself, Moody had observed the power of music over the years. Impressed by the musical talent of a US Treasury employee named Ira Sankey, Moody started actively recruiting the singer. Sankey had initially agreed to join Moody in his work in Chicago.[23] Together they formed a sort of gospel duo, Sankey singing the gospel and Moody preaching it. This signaled the start of a remarkable partnership that would influence evangelicalism in both the US and UK and serve as a model for future revivalists.

During his previously mentioned trip to the United Kingdom, Moody was invited by several prominent local clergy to return and preach a series of meetings. As a result, Moody, now accompanied by Sankey, returned to the United Kingdom in 1873. Despite facing some early challenges, the pair slowly won people's acceptance, and their popularity grew steadily.[24] British newspapers began printing his sermons and Moody's fame grew. Moody and Sankey remained in the United Kingdom until 1875, preaching throughout England, Scotland, and Ireland. Their tour culminated in a four-month stay in London, where approximately 2.5 million people attended the meetings.[25]

This tour was truly remarkable! It is hard for us to imagine, but Moody managed to speak to crowds of up to 20,000 people without any sound system, even at times from rooftops or temporary halls. The setting and absence of microphones make these meetings doubly incredible.

This marked just the start of several tours across the United Kingdom. Moody returned in September 1881 and remained until summer 1882. In the fall of 1882, he returned to Cambridge University for a student crusade. The following fall, he returned to London for a series of meetings from November 1883 to January 1884, drawing large crowds and reaching an estimated 2 million people.[26] Moody would go on a third tour of the United Kingdom from 1891 to 1892.

Not only would these tours have a spiritual impact, but they would also affect the poor in the United Kingdom for many years afterward.

Charitable Work in the United Kingdom

During the UK tours, Moody founded numerous charitable organizations and supported dozens of existing ones.

One example is his impact in Glasgow, Scotland. Historian David Bebbington has described the various charitable efforts that emerged from Moody's work there. One of the most prominent was the Glasgow Tent Hall. The Tent Hall was built in 1876 for the United Evangelical Association, which had been meeting since 1874 in a mission tent on Glasgow Green. The Association was heavily involved in the Temperance movement. On Saturday evenings, the Association in the Tent Hall offered the alternative entertainment of lantern slide shows that illustrated the evils of alcohol. The Tent Hall also hosted the Sabbath Morning Free Breakfast and the Glasgow Poor Children's Sabbath Dinner. Other charities were the Poor Children's Day Refuges, where children were cared for while their parents were at work, and the Crippled Children's League of Kindness, in which West End children were individually linked with East End children with disabilities. There were also the Weary Workers' Rest at Dunoon, the Homes for Destitute Children at Saltcoats, a rescue home for girls in danger of going astray, the Poor Children's Fresh-Air Fortnight Homes, and William Quarrier's Orphan Homes of Scotland.[27] Bebbington also points out that "a group of men associated with the Glasgow campaign threw themselves into politics to achieve Christian objectives."[28] In 1898, after surveying the impact of Moody's work in Glasgow, Sir George Adam Smith concluded that Moody's efforts had been a great force for civic righteousness in Glasgow.[29]

The story in Edinburgh was similar, but in this case, the focus was on an established ministry, Carrubber's Close Mission. Moody was introduced to Carrubber's in 1883. Moody would have been particularly interested in the ministry, as it started as a Sunday school in 1858. By the time Moody arrived, it had evolved and included "almost every form of Christian enterprise and philanthropy. Every age and class were embraced in their mission."[30] Deeply impressed with their work, Moody decided to help expand their facilities. After raising funds, Moody delivered a sermon at the laying of the cornerstone of their new building before leaving Edinburgh.[31] By the time of his death, Moody was responsible for many such mission halls throughout the British Isles.[32]

In England, the work had the same impact as in Scotland. For instance, Moody's efforts in Liverpool led to the creation of the British Workingman Company Limited. This company operated various outlets offering affordable meals, aiming to provide working people with a choice outside saloons, which was especially important for those seeking to avoid alcohol. Starting in Liverpool, the company then expanded across the United Kingdom.[33]

Following the success of their tour of the United Kingdom and Ireland, they returned to the United States. They received numerous invitations to conduct citywide meetings nationwide. Moody chose to start in Brooklyn on October 31, 1875. From Brooklyn, the meetings moved on to Philadelphia, New York, and Boston. Eventually, Moody headed west to Chicago, his second home. The Chicago crusade began on October 1, 1876, in a tabernacle that seated 10,000 people. It lasted sixteen weeks, ending on January 16, 1877.

Given his beginnings, it is hard to imagine Dwight Moody would someday speak to millions throughout the British Isles and the United States. The world was beginning to see what God could do with someone totally yielded to Him.

CHAPTER 5

Education: Practical and Biblical

Come One, Come All

Starting in 1884, Moody chose to focus his preaching trips from October to April. This change came as part of a new, more intentional direction in Moody's ministry. During this period, he also ventured into education, founding four schools across the United States. In Northfield, he opened a school for underprivileged girls in 1879, followed by a school for boys in 1881 and a Bible training school in 1890. The fourth school, connected to the Chicago Evangelistic Society, was established in 1886. After his passing, the Chicago school was renamed Moody Bible Institute, honoring his legacy. Moody's expansion into education reflected his burden for poor children. As one admirer put it,

> The sight of poor boys and girls deprived of the means of education would not let him rest until he had provided some method by which their lives should be enriched and made more in accordance with Heaven's designs for them. He dotted this fair plain with houses that young men and young women should have the means of so enlarging their lives that they might be useful to their fellows.[1]

A School for Young Girls

By 1876, Moody had settled in Northfield, Massachusetts. That summer, while riding through the hills behind his house with his brother Samuel, Moody came across a small cabin. Outside, two young girls sat with their mother, braiding straw hats. Their father, an invalid, watched nearby from a couch on the porch, reading the Greek New Testament to his daughters. An educated man who had graduated from Oberlin College and taught school, he had been struck with a paralyzing illness that ended his career. Moved by the scene, Dwight and Samuel stopped to talk with the family. Hat braiding was their primary source of income, and it was evident that his daughters shared their father's intelligence.

As they departed, both Moody and Samuel felt saddened by the girls' uncertain future. They knew the nearest school offered only basic education, and the closest high school was thirteen miles away in Greenfield. Even with transport, the girls couldn't leave their family or afford tuition. This prompted Dwight and Samuel to consider establishing a school.

This encounter led to the formation of Moody's first school, the Northfield Seminary for Young Ladies, which was opened in 1879. The two girls Moody met on his ride were among the first students.

This section from the 1899 handbook describes the school's purpose:

> [T]he girls in disproportionate numbers stay at home, attend district schools for a few terms, and often live with but little society and meager opportunities fitted to stimulate their minds in healthful directions, or properly develop their

> resources . . . This is the class of girls for whom the Northfield Seminary exists: to help and encourage them, to fit them in the best way for a happy and useful life.[2]

It is worth noting, Moody's special attention to the plight of poor girls regarding education. His school placed him at the forefront of women's education. The Northfield school would be joined shortly by a school for poor boys with the opening of the Mount Hermon School for Boys across the river from the school for girls.

Reflecting Moody's burden for the poor, the schools were "restricted to those who have small means and high aims." They particularly encouraged "the attendance of those who, from the necessity of self-support or otherwise, have been providentially hindered in getting the desired education, but who would be determined to make the most of an opportunity here."[3] In his biography, William describes Mount Hermon by saying, "The school is not for rich men's sons. There have no right here. There can be no aristocracy of wealth."[4]

Both the girls' and the boys' schools were aggressively integrated. African Americans, Native Americans, and Asian Americans were actively recruited.[5]

Specifically, regarding the girls' school, after classes concluded in 1880, Moody sent Harriet Tuttle, the school's principal, to Oklahoma to invite Native American girls to attend. This effort was inspired by a meeting with a minister in Boston, who emphasized the importance of Native teachers. In response, Moody sent Tuttle to a reservation "to receive into the school a dozen [Indian women], if so many candidates might be found, free of expense to themselves. But Miss Tuttle found many more who would have been fitted and glad to go to Northfield had the way been open; and she selected sixteen, who became members of the school with the new year."[6]

A School for Boys

The boys' school was similar in many ways; the school was for the poor and racially diverse. The diversity was demonstrated during the first graduation ceremony at Mount Hermon School for Boys. As the program put it, "William Moody, who goes on to Yale College, spoke for Americans; Louis Johnson, a full-blooded Choctaw, spoke in his own language for the various Indian tribes represented in the school; Chin Loon, in full Chinese dress, spoke for his nationality, which has several representatives at Mount Hermon; Thomas N. Baker, a full-blooded Negro and a general favorite in the school, spoke for his race."[7]

The class of 1889 included students from thirty-two nations, with one of the class officers being an ex-slave from Virginia.[8]

The Moody Bible Institute

The origins of the Bible Institute in Chicago are closely connected to the city's growing social challenges. The Institute's roots can be traced, in part, to the work of Emma Dryer. Dryer was well educated and had been active in the Chicago YWCA. She later was involved with what would become Moody Memorial Church. While there, Mr. Moody encouraged her to begin a training school for women. It began in 1873. Part of the inspiration and direction for the school came from Pennefather's Deaconesses' training school. Both Dryer and Moody visited the school in the UK. Moody had first visited in 1867 and then later encouraged Dryer to study the program. The women at Pennefather's school received training to serve among the urban poor, providing Bible teaching alongside practical assistance, including sewing, cooking, and health education. Moody and Dryer's plan was to develop a school in Chicago and eventually broaden the program to include men. Dryer also secured a commitment from Moody to provide ongoing financial support, following what he believed would be a brief campaign in England.[9] But Moody became involved in other work and, in 1875, moved permanently to Northfield.

It appears, for Moody, the work with the Institute became a case of "out of sight, out of mind." Although Chicago was no longer his permanent residence, Moody remained concerned about it, and his attention would soon refocus on the school, as living conditions in Chicago deteriorated. The city suffered from severe housing and sanitation problems that led to waves of disease among the poor. There was labor unrest, marked by increased strikes and riots. Ethnic and racial tensions simmered, and lawlessness had become a serious issue.[10]

Moody increasingly worried about the worker unrest, stating in 1886, "Either these people are to be evangelized or the leaven of Communism and infidelity will assume such enormous proportions that it will break out in a reign of terror such as this country has never known."[11] In a fundraising letter from 1887, Moody states that there were more than 40,000 arrests for disorderly conduct and other crimes in 1886, resulting in jails being filled to capacity. He continued, "Of the

800,000 people of Chicago, probably not more than one-fourth attend regularly some church, Catholic or Protestant." He concludes that the youth are being engulfed in waves of "intemperance, laziness, and crime."[12]

In response, Moody revisited the idea of a Bible Institute. Building on Dryer's early school, the school aimed to train "workers from out of the ranks" of the masses "to reach the class of the people we are after." He called these workers "gap-men," individuals who could bridge the gap between the urban working poor and the educated clergy of that era.[13]

Still operating today after nearly 150 years, Moody Bible Institute has trained tens of thousands of Christian workers and missionaries. They have pastored churches, staffed rescue missions, led educational efforts, served as missionaries and missionary aviators, worked in jails, and directed many other ministries.

When he wasn't preaching, Moody spent time in Northfield studying, being with his family, or working with his schools. When he traveled for revivals, he often chose smaller cities and kept each visit to about three days. His last trip to the United Kingdom took place from 1891 to 1892. In addition to England and Scotland, Moody toured the continent, visiting France and Italy. He also visited Israel, where he preached on the Mount of Olives on Easter Sunday morning.

The Chicago World's Fair, officially known as the World's Columbian Exposition, began in 1893. Moody saw this as "an opportunity of the century." The exposition ran from May 7 to October 31 and drew about 27.5 million visitors.[14] In response, Moody organized at least 125 different meetings on Sundays. These featured a variety of speakers who preached in multiple languages. Specifically, as one biographer put it, "every variety of gospel meeting was held: men's, women's, children's meetings; temperance, soldiers', jail meetings; open-air and cottage meetings; meetings for Germans, Poles, Bohemians, French, Jews, and even for the Arabs in the Fair grounds; meetings for praise and for prayer; all-day and all-night meetings."[15] Almost two million people heard the gospel at the various meetings.[16]

We Need Literature

During the 1890s, Moody would start another ministry focused on serving the poor through publishing. The Bible Institute Colportage Association, or BICA (today known as Moody Publishers), was established in 1894. The first book was Charles Spurgeon's *All of Grace*. By Moody's death in 1899, the catalogue had expanded to include over eighty titles.[17] The primary goal was to provide quality Christian literature at a price accessible to working people. Moody believed this could lead some to faith or help strengthen the faith of others. Additionally, BICA aimed to create employment opportunities, hence the name Colportage Association. The term "colportage" refers to the sale of books and tracts by individuals known as colporteurs or colporters. Specifically, BICA employed traveling salespeople (colporters) to distribute its materials via horse and wagon. Finally, Moody used the association to fund initiatives such as free libraries in prisons, and housing for the poor.[18]

Preaching His Last Sermon

Dwight L. Moody began his final crusade in Kansas City in November 1899. Soon after, he became ill with a progressive heart disease. Moody left the campaign and went back home to Northfield where he stayed until he died on December 22, 1899. The funeral was held on December 26, with C. I. Scofield, his pastor, presiding. Memorial services were subsequently held in many major cities across the United States and Great Britain.[19]

Considering his early circumstances, Moody's achievements were remarkable. His efforts positively impacted millions, including establishing rescue missions, safe homes for women, support for people battling addiction, providing meals and clothing, offering educational opportunities for underprivileged children, and founding churches and Sunday schools. He also helped make affordable literature available to disadvantaged groups, arranged care for wounded soldiers and respectful funerals for the poor and young, and helped create jobs.

Although there may be differing opinions regarding his understanding or approach to urban issues, Moody directly addressed these challenges. The organizations and individuals affected by his work highlight his dedication to bettering conditions for the poor.

CHAPTER 6

Understanding the Cities of the 1800s

Urbanization, Industrialization, Overcrowding, and Human Failure

In order to really understand Dwight L. Moody, or for that matter, Karl Marx, it is important to try to briefly enter into their world. They lived in a time of fantastic change and incredible problems—problems never before seen in human history. These included the explosive growth of cities, factories, mass production, pollution, immigration, and racial and ethnic integration that was unimaginable in the previous century.

As a result, it is difficult for today's reader to understand what happened to the United States in the nineteenth century. Over the course of those decades, America shifted from a mainly farming society to an urban, industrial one. As a result, Moody, like many, came to see the cities as both the greatest opportunity to develop Christian civilization and the biggest threat to destroy it.

The Insights of Josiah Strong

One of the institutions most troubled by the change was the Protestant Church in America, and one of the most important

Protestant clergypersons to speak on this subject was the prominent minister Josiah Strong. Strong was a minister, author, activist, and organizer. In addition, from 1886 to 1898, Strong served as General Secretary of the Evangelical Alliance for the United States. Strong spoke for many Protestants when, in 1885, he wrote *Our Country: Its Possible Future and Its Present Crisis*. Strong identified seven "perils" he believed were facing the nation: Catholicism, Mormonism, Socialism, intemperance, wealth, urbanization, and immigration.

In terms of the cities, Strong wrote: "The city is the nerve center of our civilization. It is also the storm center." He continued, "The city has become a serious menace to our civilization." Strong was alarmed by the mass influx of immigrants in the cities, whom he viewed as a threat to the country. Strong notes multiple statistics showing how much higher the percentage of immigrants was in cities than in the rest of the country. Of particular impact on Moody was his claim that 91 percent of Chicago was composed of immigrants.[1]

Strong found a festering illness in American cities in the 1880s: massive wealth mixed with grinding poverty. He writes, "The rich are richer, and the poor are poorer, in the city than elsewhere. . . . Not only does the proportion of the poor increase with the growth of the city, but their condition becomes more wretched." Strong begins an extended description of the horror of urban slums, at one point comparing them to the middle passage of slave ships. He concludes that in New York and London one finds "such depths of woe, such utter and heart wringing wretchedness."[2]

Strong also pointed to the rise of Roman Catholicism, alcoholism, and Socialism.[3] All this led him to the conclusion that in the cities "is heaped the social dynamite; here roughs, gamblers, thieves, robbers, lawless and desperate men of all sorts, congregate; men who are ready on any pretext to raise riots for the purpose of destruction and plunder; here gather foreigners and wage-workers; here skepticism and irreligion abound."[4] The end, he feared, was ominous and near.[5]

Although there may be some doubts about Strong's interpretations, his description of the changes in America is quite insightful. He also offers helpful perspectives on what motivated both Marx and Moody.

In America, the growth of cities and their challenges started even before the Civil War. This change was already underway, but the war accelerated it. Three East Coast cities perfectly illustrate this shift. Between 1860 and 1890, Boston, Philadelphia, and New York all saw tremendous growth. But even this incredible expansion was outdone by Moody's hometown, Chicago. Founded in 1833, the city's location was both strategic and problematic. Situated at the base of Lake Michigan, it provided excellent transportation opportunities. Yet it was also a swamp. The city expanded rapidly, rising from seventeen buildings to a population of 1.7 million by 1900, making it the fifth-largest city in the world. What's truly astonishing is that Chicago achieved all this growth despite facing a devastating fire in 1871.

Many of Chicago's new residents were immigrants. Between 1860 and 1920, nearly 28,500,000 foreigners entered the American workforce. This figure was nearly equal to the country's total population in 1850.[6] By 1900, two-thirds of the urban population were immigrants. They represented a diverse mix, including Roman Catholics and Protestants from

Europe, European Jews, and Chinese. Some people left their countries because they faced hardships, while others looked for better opportunities that weren't available at home.

The largest group of immigrants was Roman Catholic. The growth of the Roman Catholic population in the nineteenth century was meteoric.[7] One historian observed that, "During the first half of the nineteenth century, the Roman Catholic Church in the United States ceased to be a persecuted, numerically insignificant body and became the largest church in the country." By the time Moody's Sunday school was in full swing, 40 percent of all churchgoers were Roman Catholics.[8]

But immigrants weren't the only people moving to the city. Many young, native-born Americans, like Dwight Moody, also moved to urban areas, eager for new opportunities. This created numerous challenges as cities struggled to handle the growing population. As factories attracted more workers, housing shortages led to overcrowding, and many newcomers faced low wages and limited access to education. Additionally, ethnic and racial prejudices increased. This tension was often worsened by labor riots, boycotts, and strikes.[9]

Working people in the 1800s faced incredibly tough conditions beyond just housing and healthcare. Employers often expected them to work twelve to fourteen hours daily, six days a week. The meatpacking industry, in particular, was harsh, with workers forced to use corners of rooms as bathrooms. A worker engaged in bone processing was at risk of developing lung disease. Without gloves, tanners frequently dealt with sores and cuts on their fingers from chemical exposure. Sadly, these dangers could lead to amputations and other serious injuries.[10] Chicago had the world's largest meatpacking plants during Moody's time there. Specifically, by 1890, the Chicago packinghouses were killing 1,500 to 2,500 steers, 6,000 to 8,000 hogs, and 6,000 to 8,000 sheep a day.[11]

One historian's description of a meatpacking plant in Cincinnati is helpful because it was typical of such facilities at the time. The plant was a sort of "human chopping-machine where the hogs were converted into commercial pork." The speed at which the hogs were dispatched was amazing. This was accomplished by developing labor divisions to form a sort of "de-assembly line." The historian remarked, "We took out our watches and counted thirty-five seconds, from the moment one hog touched the table until the next occupied its place."[12] Another packer in Chicago estimated that his plant could dress an entire steer in thirty-four minutes, reducing the time from eight to ten hours.[13] This disassembly line did not require skilled labor, reducing the men to interchangeable parts that could be easily replaced.[14]

Chicago showcased all these issues. Plagued by overcrowding and poor sanitation, Chicago suffered waves of epidemics. One historian describes the city as filled with areas of "noisome quagmires" where human waste often spilled into drinking wells. Garbage was strewn in roadside ditches. Plank streets and sidewalks crisscrossed over piles of garbage and human and animal waste. The Chicago River was the dumping ground for various manufacturing wastes, including the runoff from tanneries, packing plants, distilleries, and glue factories. The nearby "Bubbly Creek"—the South Fork of the South Branch of the Chicago River—was also a significant health concern. The slaughterhouses dumped raw sewage, animal carcasses, chemicals, and other items that caused methane to build up in the creek, causing it to sometimes literally bubble. Parts of the creek were so overrun with waste that it was partially solid in places.[15]

One prominent Chicago citizen wrote to his brother and described the river as "positively red with blood under the Rush Street bridge and down past our factory." He concluded, "What a pestilence may result from it I don't know."[16] His last comment proved prophetic. Typhoid and dysentery caused such a high death rate that many believed Chicago had the highest per capita mortality of any city in the country.

Adding to this chilling scene was a surprisingly high level of drunkenness. Chicago boasted one saloon for every 200 residents, and its second-biggest industry was liquor distilling. Considering these facts, it seems right that the Women's Christian Temperance Union picked Chicago as the location for its headquarters.[17]

This is why Moody chose Chicago; their workers and their children in Chicago motivated Moody. Their pain, suffering, and struggle gripped his soul. These uniquely urban challenges fueled the need for his ministries. Echoing Strong's understanding of the impact of cities, Moody exclaimed, "Water runs downhill, and the highest hills are the great cities. If we can stir them, we can stir the whole nation."[18] He also shared some of Strong's concerns regarding the nature of the crisis among the urban working poor. Given what we have seen, Moody's burden for the city makes perfect sense.

America wasn't alone in facing tough times. The United Kingdom also faced its own set of challenges. In the 1800s, with the Industrial Revolution accelerating, many people moved from the countryside to cities across Great Britain. Great Britain became the first urban society in history.[19] This helps explain the time and energy Moody devoted to the great cities of the United Kingdom. Like Chicago, their overwhelming problems drew Moody to help.

London, Marx's adopted home, experienced explosive growth. During the nineteenth century, greater London grew from roughly one million to well over six million, making it the largest city in the world during that period.[20]

Furthermore, like many expanding cities of the nineteenth century, London experienced its fair share of challenges. Overcrowded housing and pollution from smog became common. Poor sanitation often led to outbreaks of illness among the residents. The city also faced issues like prostitution, crime, drunkenness, and large numbers of neglected and uneducated children, all presenting ongoing concerns for the community.[21]

London was not the only place in the United Kingdom experiencing urbanization. In fact, in the nineteenth century, Glasgow, Scotland, was the fastest-growing city in Great Britain.[22] Much of Glasgow's growth was driven by Irish Catholic immigrants who arrived without established trades. They settled in the inner-city neighborhoods, which faced challenges like poor housing, periodic outbreaks of disease, ethnic tensions, poverty, alcohol-related issues, domestic violence, and labor unrest.[23]

Both Marx and Moody experienced these challenges personally. They both believed that taking action was essential to help the urban working class, but their ideas about how to do this were entirely different.

Exploitation, Socialism, and Vice

Dwight Moody was not a Socialist. However, for Moody, profit was one thing, greed was another. Moody believed in work. He believed the Bible taught that both those who work and those who cannot work through no fault of their own, deserve respect and care. Workers should be treated fairly. Children and widows need protection and support. He also believed in helping those who struggle with addiction and seek assistance. It is no coincidence that Keir Hardie, the founder of the Labour Party in the United Kingdom, traced his political ideas to the preaching of Dwight Moody.

Billy Graham would later acknowledge that connection, stating:

> When I met the former Prime Minister of Britain, Harold Wilson, he shook hands with me and said, "Oh, yes, we come by your way." I knew what he meant. Keir Hardie helped found the British Labour Party. He had been profoundly influenced by the ministry of evangelist Dwight L. Moody. Keir Hardie was an evangelist all his life and was deeply involved in helping and organizing the working poor. He founded the British Labour Party because of his social concern, out of love for Christ. And Prime Minister Wilson was a member of that British Labour Party.[24]

When receiving the Templeton award for Religion in 1982, in his acceptance speech, Graham again noted "the conversion of Keir Hardie that led to the founding of the British Labour Party."[25]

Later on, Hardie broadened his perspectives beyond Moody by embracing socialist ideas. It is likely that Moody would harbor reservations about Harold Wilson's Labour Party. What stands out is *that Moody taught others to care for the poor*! It also highlights that individuals applied Moody's message in different ways, despite Moody's strong opposition to Socialism.

A letter from an early acquaintance of Moody, Charles Goss, makes Moody's position clear. The letter written to Moody's son-in-law, A. P. Fitt, is dated November 16, 1910. In it, Goss recounts an episode where Moody and a friend "tried to rid [him] of certain socialistic views." He goes on saying, "Put together with other statements, one can safely surmise Moody is no friend of the Labor movement."[26]

However, later in his career, Moody's perspective shifted somewhat. Consequently, in the late 1880s and into the 1890s, he started speaking out against wealth and big business.[27] In 1888, he commented, "It is more profitable to have a clear conscience with God, than to have wealth gathered by defrauding the poor, and grinding the unfortunate."[28] He attacked employers in 1894, charging, "We treat our servants just about as we treat our sewing machines; if they do their work well, all right; but if they don't, we kick them out."[29] In the same year he called A. T. Stewart, a prominent New York department store owner, "supremely selfish," stating, "One of his clerks got sick and couldn't come to the store for two or three or ten weeks; his wages were cut right off." Moody continued saying Stewart thought "he wasn't responsible for aiding the clerk.'"[30]

In 1897, he directed another verbal broadside toward employers. Moody asked rhetorically, "Are you guilty of sweating your employees? Have you deprived the hireling of his wages?

Have you paid starvation wages?"[31] Again, in 1899, Moody spoke out, and it is interesting to note that he addressed the structural problem of big corporations: "What can a poor young man do nowadays, unless he goes to work for someone else who is wealthy? . . . Trusts, corporations, are bad for young men."[32] Moody believed employers should treat their workers fairly; however, he never approved of labor unrest.

Moody's comments occasionally aligned with the views of the business community; yet, Moody openly criticized the business community whenever needed, especially as his career progressed. Stanley Gundry argues that Moody questioned the values of the capitalists. He pointed out that Moody cited the "covetousness, the inordinate greed for gain" that had "fastened on the hand of Chicago, along with many another Western City." Gundry claimed Moody "censured the selfish acquisitiveness or the employers almost as severally as he condemned the laziness and dishonesty of the employees and unemployed."[33] David Bebbington agrees, writing, Moody had "criticized American employers as sharply as any social gospeler for paying starvation wages."[34] In summary, despite concerns about workers' treatment, Moody remained committed to his core belief that personal transformation and charity are the most effective means of addressing societal issues.

Moody and Race

Moody's record on race is complicated. We have seen how Moody integrated all his meetings and schools in the northern United States. However, this would be tested in the South. After the Civil War, he traveled to Georgia for a series of evangelistic meetings. Unlike previous meetings, Moody was informed that the meetings were segregated. Angered, he declared that some Southern whites "might possibly be astonished someday to see these blacks marching into the kingdom of heaven while they themselves were shut out."[35]

Southern whites were indignant, demanding that the meetings remain segregated.[36] Moody's associates argued to keep segregated meetings, warning that integrating them would lead to trouble with the attendance of Georgia's white population.[37] Moody followed their advice. In the future, when he did run meetings in the South, they were segregated until, at a series of meetings in Texas in 1895, Moody began defying Jim Crow laws and segregation, at least for a time.[38]

Moody received criticism from several leading African Americans, many of whom were sympathetic to his faith. For example, both Francis Grimke and Ida B. Wells criticized Moody's practice and his failure to speak aggressively on racial issues.[39] Perhaps this quote from an African American pastor best summarizes their criticism of Moody: In the North, he "does not allow any discrimination against his black brother," but in the South, he "has not the courage of his convictions."[40]

Slavery is evil, and Moody spoke and acted aggressively against it. Segregation and Jim Crow were wicked as well. Moody was in a position to demonstrate the evil of segregation and aggressively denounce lynching. In both cases, he waited until the end of his career to speak and act. It was a missed opportunity and a violation of his own beliefs. (For my interpretation, read *Bread and Bibles, D. L. Moody's Evangelism and Social Action*).[41]

Moody was not perfect; he was not a flawless saint. In terms of labor issues, working conditions, and racial issues, in retrospect, he could have said more earlier in his career. Moody frequently recounted his own mistakes; he didn't want to be seen as perfect but as an imperfect person seeking to serve God. As he put it, "I've had more trouble with D. L. Moody than any other man who has crossed my path."[42]

CHAPTER 7

Sin, the Gospel, and the Human Predicament

You Don't Just Need a Handout; Your Soul Needs to Be Rescued

Moody realistically faced the urbanization of Chicago and its painful results. He understood the problem firsthand, but unlike Marx, he saw it as sin, not as a social or economic issue alone; he approached these issues from a theological perspective. Specifically, Moody viewed Christianity as an "inside-out" religion. The Bible teaches that we are all born twisted; there is something wrong with us deep within our souls. That cannot be changed by manipulating the environment or managing our personal behavior—we need a change of nature. Jesus described it as a radical change, a rebirth, a total re-creation. Only God can so totally transform us. Moody believed this, and it drove his preaching and actions.[1]

Since Moody believed that urban social ills were ultimately theological in their origin, we must briefly examine his basic theological ideas. As we do, we must consider that he was a layperson with limited formal education. He was an evangelist, not a pastor or theologian. His theology is basic, practical, and focused on salvation. Moody's genius is simplicity and earnestness. In his own words, here are the key beliefs—described as Moody's "Three Rs"[2]—that shaped his understanding of these challenges: "There are three R's in the Bible: Ruin by Sin, Redemption by Christ, and Regeneration by the Holy Ghost." And as one writer put it, "According to this triad of topics, he lays out all his campaigns."[3]

Ruined by Sin

The first R was "ruined by sin." Moody believed we are born corrupted, twisted, and rebellious. Because that is our nature, we act in a corrupt, twisted, and rebellious way. We are sinners who therefore sin. Moody believed this began with the first humans, Adam and Eve, and that we inherited that nature from them. As he put it in 1870, "When I was born of my parents in 1837, I received my nature from them, and it was a very bad nature too . . . and we might trace it right back to Adam. . . . You may say the earth is a vast hospital. Every man and woman coming into it needs a physician. If you search, you will find everyone wounded. By nature, we are sinners."[4] A little over a decade later, he restated his position. "Men are all bad by nature; the old Adam stock is bad, and we cannot bring forth good fruit until we are grafted into the one True Vine."[5] In another of his published sermons, he put it this way, "I don't care where you put man, everywhere he has tried he is a failure. He was put in Eden on trial; and some men say they wish they had Adam's chance. If you had you would go down as quickly as he did."[6] Clearly, for Moody sin was a matter of human nature, not just the environment.

He believed that, because we are sinners by nature, we all sin. As he put it in one sermon titled "Tekel," he recounts the story of Belshazzar as recorded in the book of Daniel chapter 5. Moody says that all, like Belshazzar, will be weighed on the scales of God's judgment. Using the Ten Commandments, Moody systematically shows how every man and woman is found wanting when placed on the scales of God's judgment. The point is clear: all humans sin. He concludes, unless you have Christ with you when you are weighed on God's scales, as Belshazzar was, you will be found wanting.[7]

> Is there a man here who can say honestly, "I have not got a sin that I need ask forgiveness for, I haven't one thing to repent of"? A man who has broken one commandment of God is as guilty as he who has broken ten. If a man don't feel this, and come to Him repentant and turn his face from sin toward God there is not a ray of hope. Nowhere can you find one ray from Genesis to Revelation. Don't go out of this Tabernacle saying, "I have nothing to repent."[8]

Moody believed sin was the cause of the problems he saw among the urban working class. However, sin had an even more grievous effect: eternal damnation. Moody believed in hell. During his tour in the United Kingdom in 1875, Moody preached, "If I believed there was no hell, I am sure I would be off to-morrow for America" rather than "urging man to escape the damnation of hell."[9] Humans were not merely flesh and blood, we are created in the image of God and are also spiritual beings. Moody believed there is a life to come, a life with God in heaven or separated from God in hell.

This belief helps explain Moody's priorities. Evangelism must be a priority; however, it should never be undertaken alone. As we have learned, he believed the Bible demands both preaching and care for the poor; therefore, both must be done.

Redemption by Christ

The gospel provides an answer to the problem of sin we all have. It is a two-part solution. The first is what Moody called the second R, redemption by Christ or redemption by Christ's blood. Moody believed that blood is the scarlet thread that binds the two Testaments together.

Jesus' blood was the necessary price for redemption. As he put it, "The law had been broken and the penalty of death had come upon us, and it required life to redeem us."[10] Elsewhere he said, "You and I have lost life by the fall, and what we want is to get that life back that we lost, and we have it offered to us by the atonement of Christ."[11] And finally, "I tell you the moment a man breaks away from this doctrine of the blood, religion becomes a sham."[12]

In fact, for Moody, teaching on the saving role of the blood of Christ was a nonnegotiable. Preaching in London in 1875, he made his point clearly and forcefully. "If you are in a church, either Dissenting or Established, and the minister doesn't preach the blood, get out of it as Lot out of Sodom."[13]

Moody proclaimed the power of the blood of Jesus to restore the soul, "so the soul is restored to its full beauty of color when it is washed with the blood of Jesus Christ."[14] He also believed it covered sins. He told the story of a boy in Ireland who was asked by his teacher if there was "anything

God cannot do; and the little fellow said, 'Yes, He cannot see my sins through the blood of Christ.' The blood covers them."[15] In a brief but remarkable sermon titled "The Blood," Moody spent the entire sermon merely going through the Bible, arguing for the cleansing and redeeming power of Christ's blood. He ends with, "Oh! shelter yourselves behind the blood of Christ Jesus, He will save everyone who believes in Him."[16]

His concept of redemption was very basic: "Being bought back, we sold ourselves for naught, and Christ redeemed us and bought us back."[17] Humanity's only escape is through the work of Christ. As Moody explained it, "You ask me what my hope is; it is, that Christ died for my sins, in my stead, in my place, and therefore I can enter into life eternal."[18] Elsewhere in the same sermon the point was reiterated: "If you ask me what you must do to share this blessing, I answer, go and deal personally with Christ about it. Take the sinner's place at the foot of the cross. Strip yourself of all your righteousness and put on Christ's."[19] Moody argued, "If the Word of God don't teach that, it don't teach anything."[20]

Regenerated by the Holy Spirit

The final part of the solution to sin was Moody's third R: regeneration by the Holy Ghost. He believed that while the cross is an action done *for* humanity, regeneration by the Holy Spirit is an action done *to* humanity. The Holy Spirit brings about a vital change in human nature. Moody saw this as equivalent to conversion, the new birth, or being born again. He claimed, "We must be born of the Spirit, hearts must be regenerated—born again." He believed that every conversion was a supernatural work done by God.[21]

Moody saw this as a crucial doctrine. As he put it, "This doctrine of the New Birth is therefore the foundation of all our hopes for the world to come. It is really the A B C of the Christian religion . . . if a man is unsound on this doctrine he will be unsound on almost every other fundamental doctrine in the Bible."[22]

Moody was also quite clear about what regeneration is not. He asserted that it is not attending church, making a resolution to change one's ways, praying, partaking of the Eucharist or being baptized.[23] For Moody, "*There must be a new creation.* Regeneration is a new creation; and if it is a new creation it must be the work of God."[24] Regeneration, as Moody understood it, was an inside-out event. It was not a reformation, but an inner transformation. We can't change the heart by simply changing our lifestyle or determining to do better. He explained it this way, "And I cannot help believing in the regeneration of man, when I see men who have been reclaimed. . . . Old things have passed away, and all things have become new. They are not reformed only, but *regenerated*—new men in Christ Jesus."[25] Conversion from the inside out was Moody's ultimate goal.

Listen as he describes regeneration. This not only explains his understanding but also reiterates why he believes external reforms will ultimately fail.

> The trouble with people is that they are trying to make the stream good while the fountain is bad. And that is why I am so opposed to all the work being put on the old man, trying to straighten out the old man and make him upright when he is bad from the crown of his head to the sole of his foot.

> It isn't patching up the old man, but it is hewing down that tree and putting a new graft in. It is entirely changed, a new creation. I have heard of reform, reform, until I am tired and sick of the whole thing. It is regeneration by the power of the Holy Ghost that we need.[26]

The three R's formed the backbone of Moody's doctrine, but the heart of his doctrine was his understanding of the love of God. The most comprehensive book on Moody's doctrine is Stanley Gundry's *Love Them In: The Proclamation Theology of D. L. Moody*, published in 1976. The title is a perfect description of Moody's doctrine. As one observer put it, "Love was the motive of his life, the essence of his religion, the center of his message, the incentive of his achievement and the secret of his power."[27] Moody called love the "crown of crowns worn by the triune God."[28] He believed it was the central Christian virtue and the key to Christian service. He said that regarding 1 Corinthians 13, the chapter on love, Christians should be "abiding in it day and night, not spending a night or a day there, but just go in there and spend all our time—summer and winter, twelve months in the year, then the power of Christ and Christianity would be felt as it never has been in the history of the world."[29]

One of his most famous sayings was, "Faith makes all things possible . . . love makes all things easy."[30] For Moody, what drove the three R's was the fact that God is love. It explains why God acted to save us. It also explains why a loving God calls us to help the last, the least, and the lost. It also explains Moody's actions.

These three R's driven by the love of God not only shaped his understanding of urban problems, but they also formed the core of his preaching. Preaching, of course, played a significant role in Moody's work. By some measures, Moody was not a great preacher; he was not articulate. He slaughtered the King's English, and he spoke outrageously fast. But Moody was incredibly effective. What made Moody effective was his earnestness and directness. Moody knew how to connect with people and spoke from his heart. The best way to demonstrate this is to let you read a couple of excerpts from his sermons. Although they are short, they illustrate his style well.

In this selection, Moody imagines a conversation between Jesus and his followers as He commands them to go into all the world to preach the gospel.

> I can imagine that when Christ said to the little band around Him, "Go ye into all the world and preach the Gospel," Peter said, "Lord, do You really mean that we are to go back to Jerusalem and preach the Gospel to those men that murdered You?" "Yes," said Christ, "go hunt up that man that spat in My face; tell him that he may have a seat in My Kingdom yet. Yes, Peter, go find that man that made that cruel crown of thorns and placed it on My brow, and tell him I will have a crown ready for him when he comes into My Kingdom, and there will be no thorns in it. Hunt up that man that took a reed and brought it down over the cruel thorns, driving them into My brow, and tell him I will put a scepter in his hand, and he shall rule over the nations of the earth, if he will accept salvation. Search for the man that drove the spear into My side, and tell him there is a nearer way to My heart than that. Tell him I

forgive him freely, and that he can be saved if he will accept salvation as a gift.[31]

Elsewhere, he preaches on the power of Christ's blood to forgive sins.

Look at that Roman soldier as he pushed his spear into the very heart of the God-man. What a hellish deed! But what was the next thing that took place? Blood covered the spear! Oh! Thank God, the blood covers sin. There was the blood covering the spear—the very point of it. The very crowning act of sin brought out the very crown act of love; the crown act of wickedness was the crowning act of grace.[32]

Finally, here are excerpts for his sermon titled, "God is Love."

God's love is deep and high; Paul says it passeth knowledge. We love a man as long as he is worthy of our love, and when he is not we cast him off; but we don't find in the Word of God that God casts off those who are not worthy of his love. If he did, there would be no one in the kingdom of God except Jesus himself. He was obedient unto death. He was worthy of love.[33]

Moody concluded with,

His love is unchangeable. He loved Judas, when Judas betrayed him with a kiss. I should have thought that love would have broken the heart of Judas. If there is a soul goes down to hell, it must go over God's love. You have to trample that love under your feet.[34]

Taken together, these three pieces show Moody's heart and the power of his earnest words.

Moody not only preached these ideas but also put them into practice when addressing the challenges faced by the urban poor. He believed that their hardships were linked to sin and pointed out particular sins that he believed played a major role in causing poverty. As mentioned before, Moody focused on intemperance and laziness as causes of poverty. He also addressed greed among the wealthy. In all these cases, Moody believed the only solution was redemption and regeneration.

Moody particularly focused on alcohol abuse. Here is an example from a sermon preached in Boston in 1877:

> It strikes me this curse of intemperance is worse even than our civil war. That cut off a great many men—ten, twenty, thirty, perhaps forty years earlier than their time; but think of the men that are being ruined body and soul by this terrible curse; and my only hope is that the nation will get their eyes open to the fact that it is a curse, and that there will be a cry going up to God. I noticed a few days ago in the papers that in Great Britain alone $600,000,000 are spent annually on strong drink, or $18 for each man, woman and child in Great Britain, and yet they are crying out there about hard times, and we are crying out about hard times in this country. I think if it were not for this cursed liquor traffic, we would not have any hard times or this bondage to intemperate habits.[35]

Writing in 1896, Moody reiterates his belief.

> Strong drink is an enemy, both to body and soul. It is reported that Sir Andrew Clarke, the celebrated London physician,

> once made the following statement: "Now let me say that I am speaking solemnly and carefully when I tell you that I am considerably within the mark in saying that within the rounds of my hospital wards today, seven out of every ten that lie there in their beds owe their ill health to alcohol. I do not say that seventy in every hundred are drunkards; I do not know that one of them is; but they use alcohol. So soon as a man begins to take one drop, then the desire begotten in him becomes a part of his nature, and that nature, formed by his acts, inflicts curses inexpressible when handed down to the generations that are to follow him as part and parcel of their being. When I think of this I am disposed to give up my profession—to give up everything—and to go forth upon a holy crusade to preach to all men, 'Beware of this enemy of the race!'" It is the most destructive agency in the world today. It kills more than the bloodiest wars. It is the fruitful parent of crime and idleness and poverty and disease.[36]

It should come as no surprise that Moody was active in the Temperance movement. Temperance was a consistent theme in his revivals. Moody was also, for a time, associated with Francis Willard, who became the president of the National Women's Temperance Union in 1879. In fact, in 1877, a full book was published that included a series of talks Moody delivered on temperance at various meetings in Boston.[37] Clearly, Moody believed that intemperance was a major factor in urban poverty.

A second sin was laziness. Moody believed laziness was antithetical to the Christian faith. He commented:

> I never knew yet a lazy man to be converted. If he was, he soon gave up his laziness. I tell you that laziness does not belong to Christ's Kingdom. I don't believe a man would have a lazy hair in his head if he was converted to the Lord Jesus Christ. If a man has been born of the Spirit of Christ, he isn't lazy.[38]

Elsewhere, he claimed, "I never knew a lazy man to become a Christian. . . . It is the devil whose workers are idlers."[39] This attitude was seen in his schools. The handbook for both the school in Northfield and the Mount Hermon School made it clear lazy students were not tolerated.[40]

Moody was particularly pointed in his comments to married men. Moody argued that the Bible teaches that a husband's responsibility is to provide for his family. He pointed to 1 Timothy 5:8: "If any provide not for his own, and especially for those of his own house, he hath denied the faith and is worse than an infidel."[41] While he always supported their families, Moody refused aid to husbands who refused to work.[42]

So, Moody frequently emphasized work in his sermons. One author attempted to summarize Moody's theology in six points. He then added a seventh: work. He wrote, "No idea receives as much attention as this idea."[43]

All of Moody's schools required students to do manual labor. Moody worked himself to exhaustion, even to the point of death. Despite experiencing chest pains for two weeks, he persisted in his campaign in Kansas City. He told a confidant that he hadn't shared his symptoms with his family, fearing they would stop him from preaching. On the first Tuesday, he mentioned his chest pain to a colleague but still refused medical attention for two hours. After consulting a doctor, he refused to stop speaking, even traveling two blocks from his hotel to the meeting hall by carriage. He preached again on Friday night but was so drained that he had to leave that same evening by train. He eventually returned to Northfield, but just over a month later, he died.[44]

Moody also attacked greed among the wealthy. He says, "If some of you fashionable people would get along with fewer dresses, and spent some of your pocket money relieving the poor, you would show a good deal more wisdom than in spending your lives like so many butterflies."[45] He lashed out against greed and covetousness that "fastened on the hand of Chicago, along with many another Western city."[46] A similar refrain was heard in 1890: "We have too much wealth and too much poverty. Why don't some of the people who have made their fortunes stop and go out into the highways and byways and help the poor? That's my idea of socialism, and it's founded on the ideas of Christ."[47] We have already seen Moody's criticism of employers and greed among business owners. Clearly, Moody saw greed as having a hand in the plight of the urban working poor.

Ultimately, Moody was motivated by the Bible and the influence he saw the Christian faith had on others. The Bible instructed him to preach the gospel, and he obeyed. It reminded him that this life is temporary and that what truly matters is eternity, so he focused on sharing the message of eternal life through faith in Jesus Christ.

The Bible also commanded him to look after widows, orphans, and the poor, so he took action personally and supported institutions that addressed these needs. Having received help from those who preached the gospel, he recognized how his life had been changed. His family also benefited from people who took God's command to care for the vulnerable seriously. The Bible explained that sin is the root cause of human suffering and death. It also provided an answer—faith in Jesus Christ—and a life committed to spreading the message and serving the poor.

CHAPTER 8

A Life Well Lived

The Unpredictability of God's Will

There is no connection between Moody's upbringing and what he accomplished for God. No one could have predicted that this rambunctious, uneducated child would preach to millions, and tens of thousands would be converted. No one could have known he would have a central place in religious history and leave behind a continuing legacy. God birthed in Moody a talent, a desire, and a future everyone who knew him as a child missed.

Taken together, these two quotes, one from him and one from his son, best summarize how Moody understood and responded to the problems of the urban working poor:

> I want to give you a motto that has been a great help to me. It was a Quaker's motto: "I expect to pass through this world but once. If, therefore, there be any kindness I can show or any good thing I can do to any fellow human being let me do it now; let me not defer nor neglect it, for I will not pass this way again."[1]

His son William described his father as follows:

> Although Mr. Moody labored on behalf of the individual, he was also interested in society. His conception of the Gospel was comprehensive and was not indifferent to man's intellectual and physical needs. He placed first emphasis on spiritual values because he insisted that the most efficacious means of reformation was through the individual.[2]

Dwight Moody was a man who sought to give himself entirely to God. Here was a man raised in poverty, with limited education. But he gave himself fully and wholly to God, and as we have seen, the results were astonishing.

Despite his popularity, one of Moody's most notable qualities was his humility. His ability to avoid the trap of ego and power is instructive. We live in a culture driven by power and personality. As the old Canon camera commercial put it, "Image is everything." For Moody, Jesus and the gospel were everything.

He knew his limitations and wasn't afraid to acknowledge them. He was especially open about his lack of formal education. Throughout his life, Moody often deferred to knowledgeable Bible teachers. He would spend hours asking questions of talented scholars. His creation of the Northfield Bible Conference was partly motivated by his desire to learn from great Bible teachers. Moody insisted he be called "Mr. Moody, not Rev. Moody." On more than one occasion, when he was introduced as Rev. Moody, he would stand up quickly and correct the speaker, emphasizing that he was simply Mr. Moody, a lay Sunday school teacher.

Over the last twenty or thirty years of my life, I have dedicated a significant amount of time studying Dwight Moody.

I recall being struck by Moody's strong refusal to attach his name to anything. Moody Bible Institute did not have his name until after he died; the same goes for The Moody Church. I have grown increasingly impressed with the wisdom Moody demonstrated in this decision. I wonder how many of us could stay humble if we were surrounded by a group of people eager to make our name famous. I believe Moody understood this and deliberately sought to protect himself from that temptation.

We have learned about his remarkable series of meetings in the United Kingdom from 1873 to 1875. Millions attended meetings. His name became a household word, and his meetings front-page news. At the final meeting, many ministers spoke, as did his friend, the great social reformer Lord Shaftesbury. Shaftesbury stated that, "Mr. Moody has forbidden us to praise him," as a condition of their speaking. They would, however, be permitted to praise God for using him.[3] I was struck by how Moody consciously and aggressively sought to keep the focus on God.

It was surprising to learn of Moody's reluctance to have his picture taken. He was very clear about his reasoning; he never wanted anything to be about him. One biographer explained that during one of Moody's visits to London, he turned down an offer of £1,000 to sit for his photograph. Moody was, in fact, indignant because it did not seem right.[4] However, newspaper reporters flocked to him for interviews when he became well known. During the interviews, he would spend much of the time quoting Scripture because he wanted to focus on God. This was at the core of Moody's approach to ministry: Dwight Moody was focused on making it about Jesus and the gospel.

Jesus was his "brand."

Moody was also assertive about sharing his meetings. There are stories of Moody walking into meetings and announcing to a colleague that *he* (and not Moody) would be speaking that evening; and on at least one occasion, Moody waited until his colleague was on the platform before informing him. No doubt Moody's associates knew they might be called on to preach at a moment's notice. R. A. Torrey noted, "Mr. Moody loved to keep himself in the background. At his conventions at Northfield, or anywhere else, he would push the other men to the front and, if he could, have them do all the preaching."[5]

Consequently, he was also profoundly collaborative. Moody never competed with other ministries. He trusted God to use others and looked for places without any Christian work. When Moody ran city revivals, he aggressively sought collaboration with the local churches. Moody repeatedly described his goal as serving the church, not replacing it. He started ministries and turned them over to others. This attitude explains why a broad spectrum of churches and Christian leaders so widely admired him.

Also remarkable was Moody's attitude toward money, and he lived his commitment to charity. R. A. Torrey wrote:

> Mr. Moody might have been a wealthy man, but money had no charms for him. He loved to gather money for God's work; he refused to accumulate money for himself. He told me during the World's Fair that if he had taken, for himself, the royalties on the hymnbooks which he had published, they would have amounted, at that time, to a million dollars. But Mr. Moody refused to touch the money. He had a perfect

> right to take it, for he was responsible for the publication of the books and it was his money that went into the publication of the first of them. . . . Millions of dollars passed into Mr. Moody's hands, but they passed through, they did not stick to his fingers.[6]

When looking back on Moody's life, one faces some challenges. First, it is the tendency to reduce humans to two-dimensional beings, presenting them as either sinners or saints. Second, hindsight is always 20/20. America was experiencing the complexity of urban problems for which there was no simple answer. Literally tens of thousands of books and essays have been written seeking to understand all these changes and their impact on American life. Consequently, all of these must be acknowledged as we try to understand Moody's life and work.

Some have pointed out that Moody received donations from prominent capitalists of his era.[7] He admired business leaders and appeared eager to associate with them. D. W. Whittle, a trusted confidant and William Moody's father-in-law, once noted that some could see Moody's strong desire to collaborate with the rich and powerful as a flaw. After all, some of these wealthy individuals mistreated their workers or had hidden motives for supporting Moody. However, we have seen, especially later in his career, how Moody addressed issues of greed, monopolies, and working conditions. David Bebbington puts it best, writing that while it is true that "in 1887, Chicago businessmen regarded his evangelistic training school as a cheap way of counteracting Socialism, but Moody did not set out to keep the workers in their place. In Britain, in fact, he was thought to be a dangerous subversive, championing the common man against his natural superiors."[8] Further, regardless of the motives of all his supporters, Moody was forthright about his.

You'll recall that Bebbington also stated that though "Moody reinforced the existing link between revivalism and social reform," he was not a social conservative, and "he frequently insisted that there must be public display of the fruits of the faith, and he was associated with many of the progressive causes of his day."[9] He also had friends like F. B. Meyer and Charles Spurgeon, who, as pastors, discussed social and political matters more openly than he did. He even had a following among Social Gospel advocates.

Social Gospelers were Christians (almost all Protestants) who believed that God's kingdom could be established on earth now. They all believed that building the kingdom on earth now was a central teaching of Jesus. Consequently, they believed the Christian must stop focusing only on individual sin and work to create a Christian society where the ethics of Jesus controlled all institutions in the culture. So "conversion" involved a life-changing event that motivated the person to work for the regeneration of society. Some were also captivated by liberal biblical scholarship and questioned some of the supernatural beliefs of Christianity, such as the virgin birth and miracles.[10]

Most notable was Moody's youngest son, Paul. Paul was active in the Social Gospel movement. He would go on to lead Middlebury College for twenty-one years. The college would reflect Paul's commitment to the movement and his increasing identification with more liberal strands of Protestantism. (As an aside, Moody's oldest son, William, would become a theological conservative.)

Additionally, Washington Gladden, who is considered the father of the Social Gospel movement, was a friend of Moody.[11] Moody had Gladden speak at the Northfield Bible Conferences.[12] Walter Rauschenbusch, the definitive Social Gospeler, translated, compiled, and edited a German-language hymnal, *Evangeliums-Lieder 1 und 2* (Gospel Hymns), containing the hymns of Ira Sankey, for German-speaking churches. Eventually, he would collaborate with Sankey on four hymnals.[13] Moody would use Rauschenbusch's hymnbooks at the German-speaking meetings he held at the World's Fair in Chicago. In fact, Rauschenbusch had been influenced by Moody as a young man.[14] Still, it would be a mistake to assume Moody approved of their beliefs and actions in full. The same applies to the industrialists. Moody did not fit nicely into any special category of social movements.

Moody did support men in the United Kingdom who addressed structural evil—specifically, Lord Shaftesbury. Shaftesbury passed legislation to limit working hours, worked on sanitary reforms, fought for improvements in the care of the mentally ill and in housing conditions for the poor and ragged, established schools for poor children, and pursued a host of other social causes.[15]

From today's perspective, his view of the causes of urban poverty was overly simple; while alcohol and laziness contributed to crises, the issue was more complex. In some ways, Moody did not fully understand sin. Sin is a destructive disease affecting individuals, institutions, and social structures, something Moody often overlooked. Consequently, he focused mainly on individual solutions rather than addressing structural evil.

However, these criticisms must be balanced by what Moody accomplished. Moody was deeply committed to acting in line with the Bible and his personal faith. As Bebbington put it, "Dwight L. Moody encouraged ventures of social concern among those who looked to him for guidance."[16] Those who wish to criticize him must remember that efforts for the poor were remarkable. It would be unfair to ignore his schools for the impoverished, his work with orphans, the families he fed, the jobs he created, the funerals he arranged, and his work with prisoners, prostitutes, alcoholics, and other addicts. What Moody did practically for the poor is impressive. If every Christian today followed Moody's example in caring for the poor, the world would be a very different place.

I am reminded of an anecdote from Moody himself. One day, a lady criticized Moody for his methods of evangelism in trying to win people to the Lord. Moody's reply was, "I agree with you. I don't like the way I do it either. Tell me, how do you do it?" The lady replied, "I don't do it." Moody retorted, "Then I like my way of doing it better than your way of not doing it." Whatever his flaws, he fed, clothed, and educated thousands and, by extension, millions. He made life better for untold numbers.

Moody saw social issues more clearly as he aged and spoke more openly about them later in his career.[17] It is not clear why Moody chose to speak on more issues, but his message remained the same. He insisted that conversion was ultimately the only solution, regardless of the problem.

Dwight Moody was a man of great faith, who was fully dedicated to God. We've learned about his extraordinary ministry, and his legacy is almost immeasurable. Few people in the history of the church have served more faithfully and with more impact. But no human being is flawless, and this should not be surprising; the Bible is full of stories of godly men and women who faltered during tests: Abraham, Sarah, Moses, David, and Peter, to name a few. It is also good news to all of us—God uses imperfect people!

Having studied Moody for years, I can say with certainty that he would have been disappointed with any book about him that did not ultimately point to Christ. For Moody, his life story is not a list of accomplishments and failures; it is a testimony to the grace of God. To conclude without reminding us of his faith would be wrong. Moody would say to all who read this book, do not look at me, look at Christ!

Moody was right about Christ and the gospel. We cannot save ourselves; sin is too powerful, and death claims us all. There is something profoundly wrong with us and our world. No amount of social reform can prevent death or eliminate evil. Jesus Christ alone conquered death, and only He offers forgiveness and eternal hope. Moody called everyone to turn to Christ for the ultimate salvation He alone can provide. He was also right to call Christians to serve the poor.

Now in the final segment of this book, let us go to the tombstone of Karl Marx and briefly contemplate his tragic legacy. We will compare it with the tombstone of D. L. Moody (and that of his dear wife Emma). One man defied God; the other took the advice of Henry Varley, "The world has yet to see what God can do through a man who is totally surrendered to Him."

The contrast is as different as time and eternity, heaven and hell. And finally, we will ask: What will our legacy be?

Two Tombstones, One Choice

What Epitaph Will Be on Our Tombstone?

by Erwin Lutzer

What did Karl Marx and Dwight L. Moody leave behind, and what should we learn from them?

Even as we contemplate their legacies, a powerful lesson for us as parents comes to mind: You have no idea who you are raising and what their impact in life will be. Heinrich and Henriette Marx died not knowing that their son Karl would bring destruction to much of the world. And Betsy Moody and her alcoholic husband, who died when their son Dwight was eight, had no idea they were raising a child who would bless the world through his preaching and leave a legacy of educational institutions and a church in Chicago that still help spread the gospel around the world. Let us be careful and prayerful as we raise our children.

We make many choices in life; but the reality is that we have only one real, life-altering choice: What direction will we take with our lives, and where we will spend eternity? Then we must ask: What will we leave behind? What is our legacy? What will those left behind really think and say of us? Not the beautiful words that may be said at our eulogy, but rather the impact of our lives. All choices have consequences, and we must make our decisions with the end in mind.

So come with us to the graves of both Marx and Moody to see if we can find the clue to what they left behind. And then ask what should be written on our own tombstone . . .

At the Grave of Karl Marx

We were accompanied by a camera crew the morning we arrived at the tomb of Karl Marx in Highgate Cemetery in London, England, on a cool morning in June. Since then, having studied more carefully Karl Marx's upbringing, his societal (and even demonic) influences, and his rejection of God, I now understand more clearly why our tour guide (who made it clear he was not a Christian believer) quipped, "There are rumors that Karl comes out at night and wanders around the cemetery." Though this is just superstition, there is something even more sinister about the "ghost" of Karl Marx—his writings have released the demons of repression, violence, death, and extreme poverty around the globe.

I've heard many commentators surmise that Marx would be scandalized if he saw the devastation his theories had unleashed on the world; he would not have thought his bold demand to "forcibly overthrow all of existing society" would actually be implemented. I beg to differ; I think that if he were alive, Marx might take delight in the devastation his writings unleashed. Of course we must leave those matters for God to judge. All we know is that he proclaimed a message that caused massive destruction in many countries of the world.

On his tombstone are two quotations, displayed prominently; the more visible near the top of his tombstone has these famous words:

"Workers of all lands unite."

Farther below is this well-known saying:

"The philosophers have only interpreted the world in various ways; the point however is to change it."[1]

Unite around what? Change the world how?

Here is a globalist call for a world united by a humanistic, materialistic, and eventually, a godless society; a call to exalt the state above God and above individual liberties. This is a call for a worldwide revolution that would upend the present order and usher in a man-driven, hellish rule that would mean the withdrawal of freedom, the enslavement of the individual, and the killing of millions.

Unite to build a Tower of Babel that curses God and glorifies man.

Change the world? Yes, but Marx would only change it for the worse. Without accepting the reality of sin and mankind's need of redemption, he was left with no resources to lift man out of his bondage of personal and moral darkness into the light of being a child of God. Marx was in effect a spiritually blind man leading other blind men toward personal and national destruction.

As we know, his legacy was one of hate and division, leaving millions of people massacred and tortured from the resulting multiplication of evil. We can also credit him with contributing to the destruction of the family, exacerbating hatred between classes of people, and misleading whole countries into an abyss of condemnation. As Paul said, "Professing themselves to be wise, they became fools, and changed the glory of the uncorruptible God into an image made like to corruptible man" (Rom. 1:22–23 KJV).

When Satan came to Jesus and offered Him all the kingdoms of the world if He bowed down and worshiped him, Jesus, of course, refused the offer and said, "You shall worship the Lord your God and him only shall you serve" (Matt. 4:10). I believe Marx took Satan's original offer. He joined the devil to destroy as much of this world as possible. And like Faust, he made a pact with the devil, hoping for vindication in the end.

Do not forget the words of Mephistopheles, "All that has come into existence deserves to be destroyed." Again, I point out the words of Revelation 9:11, where we read that the angel of the bottomless pit is called Abaddon in Hebrew and Apollyon in Greek, both words meaning *destroyer*. Marx could only destroy; he could not build.

If I had the authority to change the wording on Marx's tombstone it would read,

"Thus says the LORD: 'Cursed is the man who trusts in man and makes flesh his strength, whose heart turns away from the LORD. He is like a shrub in the desert, and shall not see any good come. He shall dwell in the parched places of the wilderness, in an uninhabited salt land'" (Jer. 17:5–6).

A tragic legacy.

At the Graves of Mr. and Mrs. D. L. Moody

On Round Top in Northfield, Massachusetts, are two graves; the grave of D. L. Moody and his wife, Emma, a wonderful helpmeet who, it is said, was his balance wheel; she was a wise woman with whom he had five children. Without

Emma, Moody's legacy would not be the inspiration it is to all of us today.

His wife Emma's tombstone has the inscription: "His servants shall serve him . . . and they shall reign for ever and ever" (Rev. 22:3, 5 KJV). Can there be a greater honor than to both serve Christ in this life and reigning with Him for all of eternity? It is a reminder that God through Christ plucked us up from the mire and set us on marble; He took us from the pit of our sin and set us in the palace. What a future, and what a legacy Emma left behind.

Next to her is the gravestone of her husband Dwight with a snatch of his favorite verse, "He that doeth the will of God abideth forever" (1 John 2:17 KJV). The full verse reads, "The world passeth away, and the lust thereof: but he that doeth the will of God abideth for ever."

Yes, Moody's life and the impact of his ministry will abide forever. The gospel he preached brought people into the kingdom of God and the joy of eternal life. And even today his ministry is still remembered in cities abroad where he and Sankey introduced the gospel in word and in song. While visiting the great St. Giles Church in Edinburgh, I told the tour guide I was from The Moody Church. "You mean the Moody who had meetings throughout the British Isles with Sankey? . . . We still have a Sankey/Moody hymnal in our home . . . and my grandmother used to talk about them."

Moody died not knowing that 130 years later, his impact would continue in the lives and institutions he left behind. Like a pebble thrown into a pond, the ripples go on for all eternity. "Blessed are the dead who die in the Lord . . . for their deeds follow them!" (Rev. 14:13).

In contrast to Marx, we can summarize Moody's life also by a verse from Jeremiah 17: "Blessed is the man who trusts in the Lord, whose trust is the Lord. He is like a tree planted by water, that sends out its roots by the stream, and does not fear when heat comes, for its leaves remain green, and is not anxious in the year of drought, for it does not cease to bear fruit" (Jer. 17:7–8).

The contrast between Marx and Moody is between a shrub in the desert and a tree planted by the water. Hell and heaven; destruction and everlasting life.

Two different gospels, two different destinies, two very different eternities.

Our Tombstone and Our Legacy: Choose Today

We can't avoid eternity, but we can plan for it.

Supposing you died today; in a single phrase, summarize what *should* be written on your tombstone. I'm not speaking about some beautiful saying a friend or relative might write, but rather what phrase truly would summarize your life? It is not about what others say about you, but rather what you know to be true about you. Before we get to our legacy, let's consider a few of the biblical characters and how their lives can be encapsulated.

Biblical Legacies

In the Bible, there are many legacies recorded—some good and some not so good. Below are just a few examples:

Caleb, one of the spies who believed God would help the Israelites capture the land from the Canaanites—God's verdict of him: "He has a different spirit and has followed me fully" (Num. 14:24).

King Saul, who clung to the kingdom even when God declared him unqualified, admitted, "I have played the fool, and have erred exceedingly" (1 Sam. 26:21 KJV).

King David, whose grievous sin left a mixed legacy, yet given the psalms he wrote and love he had for God, we might summarize his life, thusly: "One thing I have asked of the LORD, that will I seek after: that I may dwell in the house of the LORD: to gaze upon the beauty of the LORD and to inquire at his temple" (Ps. 27:4).

King Solomon, who received wisdom from God but ended up with many foreign wives and worshiping their pagan gods: "His wives turned away his heart after other gods, and his heart was not wholly true to the LORD his God" (1 Kings 11:4).

Mary, who washed the feet of Jesus and anointed them with precious oil—Jesus commended her: "She has done a beautiful thing to me . . . she has done what she could" (Mark 14:6, 8).

Judas, who betrayed Jesus—Jesus said of him: "It would have been better for that man if he had not been born" (Matt. 26:24).

Paul the apostle's testimony: "I have fought the good fight, I have finished the race, I have kept the faith" (2 Tim. 4:7).

Your Legacy and Mine

From Genesis to Revelation, the Bible presents us with only one choice that determines our eternal destiny: "Whoever believes in the Son has eternal life; whoever does not obey the Son shall not see life, but the wrath of God remains on him" (John 3:36). Jesus explained that there are two divergent paths and warned, "Enter by the narrow gate. For the gate is wide and the way is easy that leads to destruction, and those who enter it are many. For the gate is narrow and the way is hard that leads to life and those who find it are few" (Matt. 7:13–14). The narrow path is hard because we must face our own sin and our need for a Savior. It is renouncing self-effort as a means of salvation and seeing that faith in Christ alone is our only hope of heaven. But in return it also leads to a life lived on Earth with purpose and meaning. "For we are his workmanship, created in Christ Jesus for good works, which God prepared beforehand, that we should walk in them" (Eph. 2:10).

Believers have an exciting future.

Utopia is on its way. It will not come about by Marx's call for a worldwide revolution, but will come to pass when Jesus our Savior returns as King of kings and Lord of lords. Descriptions of this golden age are found throughout the Bible. Christ's rule will be worldwide, with justice and peace; His return to earth will lead to an eternal kingdom, where the redeemed of all the ages will serve Him with joyful worship.

The Old Testament prophet Isaiah predicted that Jesus would be born and "the government shall be upon his shoulder, and he shall be called Wonderful Counselor, Mighty God, Everlasting Father, Prince of Peace. Of the increase of his government and of peace there will be no end, on the throne of David and over his kingdom to establish it and to uphold it with justice and with righteousness from this time forth and forever more. The zeal of the LORD of hosts will do this" (Isa. 9:6–7).

Jesus explained: "When the Son of Man comes in his glory and all the angels with him. . . . Then the King will say to those on his right, 'Come you who are blessed by my Father, inherit the kingdom prepared for you from the foundation of the world' (Matt. 25:31–34).

So, let me ask: Will our legacy be based on time or eternity? Will we run the race focusing on earthly lusts or will we "seek the things that are above, where Christ is, seated at the right hand of God. Set your minds on things that are above, not on things that are on earth. For you have died and your life is hidden with Christ in God. When Christ who is your life appears, then you also will appear with him in glory" (Col. 3:1–4).

Since we are all on a path to eternity, the question is: what are our priorities? What influences have we left behind? How will we be remembered? What *should* be on our tombstone? Here are some honest suggestions.

He/She loved money.
He/She lived for pleasure.
He/She reveled in their addictions.
He/She was always angry.
Or:
He/She sacrificed for others.
He/She prayed fervently and consistently.
He/She loved to share the gospel.
He/She said, "For me to live is Christ, and to die is gain."
He/She loved and served the Lord their God with all their soul and mind.

Every human being leaves a legacy, whether good, bad, or indifferent. In some way, the world will be at least a very little bit different because of the impact we will leave behind. We should think of our lives as one long gift to the next generation. What we leave behind really matters.

A question to ponder: If you continue on the path you are on today, where will it lead you? We are all on a journey to somewhere, and sincerity in the wrong direction will not help us. Faithfulness to Christ and the gospel must be our daily goal.

As the lyrics challenge us in the song "Find Us Faithful":

> We're pilgrims on the journey of the narrow road
> And those who've gone before us line the way
> Cheering on the faithful, encouraging the weary
> Their lives a stirring testament to God's sustaining grace
> Surrounded by so great a cloud of witnesses
> Let us run the race not only for the prize
> But as those who've gone before us
> Let us leave to those behind us
> The heritage of faithfulness passed on through godly lives
>
> Oh, may all who come behind us find us faithful
> May the fire of our devotion light their way
> May the footprints that we leave lead them to believe
> And the lives we live inspire them to obey
> Oh, may all who come behind us find us faithful.[2]

"Therefore, my beloved brothers, be steadfast, immovable, always abounding in the work of the Lord, knowing that in the Lord your labor is not in vain" (1 Cor. 15:58).

The only thing that really matters is what matters forever.

Acknowledgments

Both of us as authors want to thank our wives for their support in this writing project. Without their patience during our long hours on a computer, with a notebook at our side, this project could never have been completed. Thank you and thank you!

We also want to thank the leadership of Moody Publishers. Thanks, Randall, publisher, for accepting our idea and motivating us with regular encouragement. Drew, acquisitions editor, we appreciated both your feedback and keeping us on schedule. And Amanda, you edited the manuscript with the same care, diligence, and high standards we have come to expect. Thanks for patiently reading our emails and answering our many questions.

We express our appreciation to the entire Moody Publishers team that works with dedication to get the gospel around the world.

Notes

Part One: Karl Marx

Chapter 1: My Visit to Two Graves

1. Karl Marx and Friedrich Engels, *Marx/Engels Collected Works*, *Volume 45: Letters 1874–1879* (Lawrence & Wishart, 1989), 311–14.
2. Quoted in James Lutzweiler, *The Roots of Billy Graham: Dwight L. Moody in Charlotte, North Carolina, March 8–17, 1893* (Schnappsburg University Press, 2002), 5.
3. William J. Federer and R. Michael Federer, *Courageous Christianity: How a 19th century revival sparked the Muscular Christianity movement, Y.M.C.A. athletics, and a youth-led race to save the world* (Amerisearch, Inc., 2025).
4. *Karl Marx and Friedrich Engels: Collected Works, Volume 43: Letters 1868–1870* (Lawrence & Wishart, 2010); digital edition, 541). See also: https://marxists.architexturez.net/archive/marx/works/1868/04/01.htm.
5. *Collins Dictionary*, "Verabscheuen," https://www.collinsdictionary.com/dictionary/german-english/verabscheuen.
6. Karl Marx and Friedrich Engels, *Marx/Engels Collected Works, Volume 24* (Progress Publishers; Lawrence & Wishart; International Publishers, 1989), 467–68.
7. Ibid.
8. Ibid.
9. Ibid.
10. Philip S. Foner, ed., *Karl Marx Remembered: Comments at the Time of His Death* (Synthesis Publications, 1983), 10.

11. Ibid., 18.

Chapter 2: A Father and Mother's Concern for Their Son

1. *The Unknown Marx: Documents concerning Karl Marx,* trans. and ed. Robert Payne (New York University Press, 1971), 41.
2. Karl Marx and Friedrich Engels, *Marx/Engels Collected Works*, *Volume 1* (Lawrence & Wishart, 2010), 670. See also: https://archive.org/details/collected-works-karl-marx-Friedrich-engels-collected-works-vol.-1/page/670/mode/2up.
3. William Ernest Henley, "Invictus," (1875), Britannica, https://www.britannica.com/biography/William-Ernest-Henley#ref215876.
4. Johann Wolfgang von Goethe, *Faust I & II*, ed. and trans. Stuart Atkins, vol. 2 of *Goethe: The Collected Works in 12 Volumes* (Princeton University Press, 1994), lines 1339–40.
5. Karl Marx, "Letter to His Father, 10 November 1837," in *Karl Marx and Friedrich Engels: Collected Works*, trans. Clemens Dutt, vol. 1, Karl Marx: 1835–1843 (Progress Publishers; Lawrence & Wishart; International Publishers, 1975), 18.
6. Robert Payne, *Marx: A Biography* (W. H. Allen & Co., 1968), 52.
7. Heinrich Marx, "Letter from Heinrich Marx to Son Karl," 9 December 1837, in *Karl Marx and Friedrich Engels: Collected Works*, trans. Clemens Dutt, vol. 1, Karl Marx: 1835–1843 (Progress Publishers; Lawrence & Wishart; International Publishers, 1975), 685–91.
8. Paul Johnson, *Intellectuals* (Harper & Row Publishers, 1990), 74.
9. Fulton J. Sheen, *The Church, Communism and Democracy* (Dell Publishing Co., Inc., 1964), 140.
10. Jonathan Sperber, *Karl Marx: A Nineteenth-Century Life* (Liveright Publishing Corporation, 2013), 256.
11. Karl Marx and Friedrich Engels, *The Communist Manifesto* (International Publishers, 2024), 30.
12. Karl Marx, "Letter to Friedrich Engels in Manchester, 2 August 1862," in *Karl Marx, Friedrich Engels: Collected Works*, trans. Peter and Betty Ross, vol. 41, Karl Marx and Friedrich Engels 1860–1864 (Progress Publishers; Lawrence & Wishart; International Publishers, 1985), 401.
13. Paul Kengor, *The Devil and Karl Marx* (TAN Books, 2020), 72. See also, Paul Johnson, *Intellectuals* (Harper & Row, Publishers, 1990), 73.

14. Ibid.

15. See Francis Wheen, *Karl Marx* (Fourth Estate Limited, 1999), 385–86.

Chapter 3: A Revolutionary in the Making

1. Friedrich Engels, "A Fragment," in *Karl Marx and Friedrich Engels: Collected Works*, trans. Clemens Dutt, vol. 2, Karl Marx: 1835–1843 (Progress Publishers; Lawrence & Wishart; International Publishers, 1975), 555–56. See also Friedrich Engels, "An mein Herz," in *Friedrich Engels: Collected Works, vol. 2 (1838–1842)* (Progress Publishers, 1975), 5.
2. Ibid.
3. Robert Payne, *Marx: A Biography* (W. H. Allen & Co., 1968), 81.
4. Karl Marx. "The Fiddler," in *Early Writings*, trans. Gregor Benton and Alex Blasing (Penguin Books/New Left Review, 1975), 7–8.
5. Karl Marx, "Human Pride," in *Early Writings*, trans. Gregor Benton and Alex Blasing (Penguin Books/New Left Review, 1975), 9.
6. Johann Wolfgang von Goethe, *Faust I & II*, ed. and trans. Stuart Atkins, vol. 2 of *Goethe: The Collected Works in 12 Volumes* (Princeton University Press, 1994), lines 1339–40.
7. Karl Marx, "The Pale Maiden," in *Early Writings*, trans. Gregor Benton and Alex Blasing (Penguin Books/New Left Review, 1975), 5–6.
8. This is a paraphrase from the original: "The time has come when we must tear God out of heaven just as we tear the capitalist out of his factories." See "Friedrich Engels to Friedrich Graeber" [Bremen, probably 28 February–2 March 1841], in: *Karl Marx Frederick Engels Collected Works (MECW), vol. 2 (1838–1842)* (Progress Publishers / Lawrence & Wishart, 1975), 525.
9. Karl Marx, "Invocation of One in Despair," in *Early Writings*, trans. Gregor Benton and Alex Blasing (Penguin Books/New Left Review, 1975), 10.
10. Karl Popper, *The Open Society and Its Enemies* (Routledge, 2012), 294.
11. Ibid.
12. Richard Wurmbrand, *Tortured for Christ* (Crossway, 1987), 36.
13. Ibid., 37.
14. Richard Wurmbrand, *Marx and Satan* (G/L Regal Books), 97.

Chapter 4: Structural Evil and the Search for a Solution

1. Karl Marx and Friedrich Engels, *The Communist Manifesto* (International Publishers, 2024), 9.
2. Ibid., 11.
3. Quoted in James Lutzweiler, *The Roots of Billy Graham: Dwight L. Moody in Charlotte, North Carolina, March 8–17, 1893* (Schnappsburg University Press, 2002), 5.
4. Marx and Engels, *The Communist Manifesto*, 8.
5. Ibid.
6. See Friedrich Engels' preface to *The Communist Manifesto*, Karl Marx and Friedrich Engels, *The Communist Manifesto* (International Publishers, 2024), 3–7.

Chapter 5: The Gospel of Marxism

1. Karl Marx and Friedrich Engels, *The Communist Manifesto* (International Publishers, 2024), 23.
2. Ibid., 24.
3. Ibid., 25.
4. Ibid.
5. Karl Marx, "Critique of the Gotha Programme," in *Karl Marx Friederich Engels Collected Works, vol. 24, Marx and Engels: 1874–1883*, trans. Richard Dixon et al. (Progress Publishers, 1989), 87.
6. Karl Marx, "Contribution to the Critique of Hegel's Philosophy of Right: Introduction," in *Karl Marx Frederick Engels Collected Works, vol. 3, Marx and Engels: 1843–1844*, trans. Jack Cohen et al. (Progress Publishers, 1975), 175.
7. Karl Marx, "Letter to Friedrich Engels in Manchester, 2 August 1862," in *Karl Marx, Friedrich Engels: Collected Works*, trans. Peter and Betty Ross, vol. 41, Karl Marx and Friedrich Engels 1860–1864 (Progress Publishers; Lawrence & Wishart; International Publishers, 1985), 401.
8. Marx and Engels, *The Communist Manifesto*, 27.
9. Friedrich Engels, *The Origin of the Family, Private Property and the State*, trans. by Ernest Untermann (Charles H. Kerr & Company, 1902), 149.

10. This story is recounted in Paul Johnson's *Intellectuals* (Harper & Row, Publishers, 1990), 79–81.

11. Paul Kengor, *The Devil and Karl Marx* (TAN Books, 2020), 72. See also, Paul Johnson, *Intellectuals* (Harper & Row, Publishers, 1990), 102. See also, Friedrich Engels, "The Origin of the Family, Private Property and the State," in *Karl Marx Frederick Engels Collected Works, vol. 26, Engels: 1882–1889*, trans. Richard Dixon et al. (Progress Publisher, 1990), 129–276, esp. 164–65.

12. Friedrich Engels, "The Origin of the Family, Private Property and the State," in *Karl Marx Frederick Engels Collected Works, vol. 26, Engels: 1882–1889*, trans. Richard Dixon et al. (Progress Publisher, 1990), 164.

13. Marx and Engels, *The Communist Manifesto*, 29.

14. "The Declaration of Independence," National Archives, https://www.archives.gov/founding-docs/declaration-transcript.

15. Marx and Engels, *The Communist Manifesto*, 44.

16. Ibid., 44.

17. Karl Marx, "Letter to Joseph Weydemeyer, February 22, 1852," in *Karl Marx Friederich Engels Collected Works, vol. 39, Letters 1852–1855,* trans. Peter and Betty Ross (Progress Publishers; Lawrence & Wishart; International Publishers, 1983), 60–66.

18. Marx and Engels, *The Communist Manifesto*, 44.

19. Ibid., 28.

20. Ibid., 30.

21. The 2019 Revolution Festival was hosted by the International Marxist Tendency (IMT), which is a Trotskyist organization with sections in over 30 countries, including the US, UK, and Canada. To Svensson's keynote address, see "Why Marxists must fight for open borders," Marxist.com, March 10, 2020. https://marxist.com/video-why-marxists-must-fight-for-open-borders.htm.

22. W. Cleon Skousen, *The Naked Communist: Exposing Communism and Restoring Freedom* (Izzard Ink Publishing, 2017), 29.

Chapter 6: Marxism Applied: Criminals Needed

1. Thomas Sowell, *Social Justice Fallacies* (Basic Books, 2023), 98.

2. Johann Wolfgang von Goethe, *Faust I & II*, ed. and trans. Stuart Atkins, vol. 2 of *Goethe: The Collected Works in 12 Volumes* (Princeton University Press, 1994), lines 1339–40.

3. W. Cleon Skousen, *The Naked Communist: Exposing Communism and Restoring Freedom* (Salt Lake City: Izzard Ink Publishing, 2017), 29–30.

4. Ibid., 31.

5. Vladimir Lenin, Graduation Certificate, Simbirsk Classical Gymnasium, May 1887. Reproduced in *Lenin: A Biography* (official Soviet edition) (Progress Publishers, 1966), plate between 32–33.

6. Paul Kengor, *The Devil and Karl Marx* (TAN Books, 2020), 72. See also, Paul Johnson, *Intellectuals* (Harper & Row, Publishers, 1990), 110.

7. V. I. Lenin, "Socialism and Religion," December 3, 1905. See Marxists .org, https://www.marxists.org/archive/lenin/works/1905/dec/03.htm.

8. Quoted in Dmitri Volkogonov, *Lenin: A New Biography*, trans. and ed. Harold Shukman (Free Press, 1994), 47.

9. Quoted in David Shub, *Lenin: A Biography* (Penguin Books, 1971), 36.

10. Rod Dreher, *Live Not by Lies* (Sentinel, 2020), 25.

11. Ibid., 52.

12. V. I. Lenin, "Letter to the Central Committee, The Moscow and Petrograd Committees and the Bolshevik Members of the Petrograd and Moscow Soviets," October 1 (14), 1917. See Marxists.org, https://www.marxists.org/archive/lenin/works/1917/oct/01b.htm.

13. George Santayana, *The Life of Reason: Reason in Common Sense* (Charles Scribner's Sons, 1905), 284.

14. Aleksandr Solzhenitsyn, *The Gulag Archipelago 1918–1956*, trans. Thomas P. Whitney and Harry Willetts; abr. Edward E. Ericson Jr. (Harper Perennial, 1983), 39.

15. Karl Marx, "Critique of the Gotha Programme," in *Karl Marx Friederich Engels Collected Works, vol. 24, Marx and Engels: 1874–1883*, trans. Richard Dixon et al. (Progress Publishers, 1989), 87.

16. Andrew Hosken and Albana Kasapi, "Albania: The Country Searching for Hundreds of Mass Graves," BBC, October 31, 2017, https://www.bbc.com/news/world-europe-41818359.

17. "Albania—The Cultural and Ideological Revolution," http://www.country-data.com/cgi-bin/query/r-170.html.

18. "Albania—Hoxha's Antireligous Campaign," http://www.country-data.com/cgi-bin/query/r-186.html.
19. Ibid.
20. Edwin Jacques and David Young, *Battle for Albania* (Wrexham: Krivine Books, 1998), 131.
21. Quoted in Jacques and Young, *Battle for Albania*, 132–33.
22. Ibid., 133.
23. George Reisman, "Why Nazism Was Socialism and Why Socialism Is Totalitarian," October 1, 2021, Mises Institute, https://mises.org/mises-daily/why-nazism-was-socialism-and-why-socialism-totalitarian.
24. Ibid.

Chapter 7: Marxism Comes to America

1. Benito Mussolini, "The Doctrine of Fascism," in *Fascism: Doctrine and Institutions* (Ardita, 1935), 11.
2. Antonio Gramsci, "Audacia e fede," *Avanti!*, May 22, 1916. Translated by the author from the original Italian text published in Antonio Gramsci, *Scritti giovanili 1914–1918* (Einaudi, 1958), 113–14.
3. Antonio Gramsci, "Workers and Peasants," in *Selections from Political Writings 1910–1920*, ed. Quintin Hoare, trans. John Mathews (International Publishers, 1990), 130–31.
4. Antonio Gramsci, *Prison Notebooks*, ed. and trans. Joseph A. Buttigieg, vol. 3 (Columbia University Press, 2007), 308–309 (Quaderno 24, § 3).
5. Ibid., 399–400 (Quaderno 16 [XXII], § 9).
6. Ingo Cornils, "'The Struggle Continues': Rudi Dutschke's Long March," in *Student Protest: The Sixties and After*, ed. Gerard J. DeGroot (Longman, 1998), 100–14, esp. 101–105.
7. Al Benson Jr., "Columbia University and the Marxists," Metropolis Café, November 15, 2019, https://metropolis.cafe/2019/11/14/benson-columbia-university-and-the-marxists/.
8. Rod Dreher, *Live Not by Lies* (Sentinel, 2020), 43.
9. *We Will Not Be Silenced* (2020) and *No Reason to Hide* (2022) were both published by Harvest House Publishers.

10. George Orwell, "As I Please," Tribune, 4 February 1944, in *The Collected Essays, Journalism and Letters of George Orwell*, vol. 3, *As I Please, 1943–1945*, ed. Sonia Orwell and Ian Angus (Secker & Warburg, 1968), 121.

11. George Orwell, *1984* (Secker & Warburg, 1949), 37.

12. Sara E. Wilson, "Arthur M. Schlesinger, Jr., National Humanities Medal, 1998," National Endowment for the Humanities, https://www.neh.gov/about/awards/national-humanities-medals/arthur-m-schlesinger-jr.

13. Nikole Hannah-Jones, "The 1619 Project," *New York Times Magazine*, August 14, 2019, https://www.nytimes.com/interactive/2019/08/14/magazine/black-history-american-democracy.html.

14. See "Declaration of Independence," National Archives, https://www.archives.gov/founding-docs/declaration-transcript.

15. Jordan Boyd, "In Racist Screed, NYT's 1619 Project Founder Calls 'White Race,' 'Barbaric Devils,' 'Bloodsuckers,' Columbus 'No Different than Hitler,'" *Federalist*, June 25, 2020, https://thefederalist.com/2020/06/25/in-racist-screed-nyts-1619-project-founder-calls-white-race-barbaric-devils-bloodsuckers-no-different-than-hitler/. Also see the original Nikole [Nicole] Hannah-Jones article here: https://www.scribd.com/document/466921269/NYT-s-1619-Project-Founder-Calls-White-Race-Barbaric-Devils-Bloodsuckers-No-Different-Than-Hitler-x#from_embed.

16. Orwell, *1984*, 78.

17. Saul Alinsky, *Rules for Radicals* (Vintage Books, 1989), ix.

18. Robin DiAngelo, *White Fragility: Why It's So Hard for White People to Talk About Racism* (Beacon Press, 2018), 21.

19. Martin Luther King, Jr., "I Have a Dream," speech delivered at the March on Washington for Jobs and Freedom, Washington, DC, August 28, 1963, in *A Call to Conscience: The Landmark Speeches of Dr. Martin Luther King, Jr.*, ed. Clayborne Carson and Kris Shepard (Warner Books, 2001), 85.

20. W. Cleon Skousen, *The Naked Communist: Exposing Communism and Restoring Freedom* (Izzard Ink Publishing, 2017), 96.

21. Theodore Dalrymple, *Life at the Bottom: The Worldview That Makes the Underclass* (Ivan R. Dee, 2001), x.

22. Ibid., xi–xii.

23. Jeffrey A. Tucker, "Why Free Speech on Campus Is Under Attack: Blame Marcuse," Foundation for Economic Education, April 24, 2017, https://fee.org/articles/why-free-speech-on-campus-is-under-attack-blame-marcuse/.

24. Herbert Marcuse, *The Essential Marcuse: Selected Writings of Philosopher and Social Critic Herbert Marcuse* (Beacon Press, 2007), 34.

25. Ibid., 45.

26. Jeffrey A. Tucker, "Why Free Speech on Campus Is Under Attack: Blame Marcuse," Foundation for Economic Education, April 24, 2017, https://fee.org/articles/why-free-speech-on-campus-is-under-attack-blame-marcuse/.

27. Ibid.

28. Ibid.

29. Herbert Marcuse, "Repressive Tolerance," https://www.marcuse.org/herbert/publications/1960s/1965-repressive-tolerance-fulltext.html.

30. Ibid.

31. Ibid.

32. This phrase was coined in the book of the same title by Richard M. Weaver, *Ideas Have Consequences* (University of Chicago Press, 1948). It is considered a foundational text of the modern conservative movement, https://press.uchicago.edu/ucp/books/book/chicago/I/bo17116688.html.

33. Tucker, "Why Free Speech on Campus Is Under Attack: Blame Marcuse."

34. Stanley Fish, *There's No Such Thing as Free Speech: And It's a Good Thing, Too* (Oxford University Press, 1994), 68.

35. Stephen R. C. Hicks, *Explaining Postmodernism: Skepticism and Socialism from Rousseau to Foucault* (Ockham's Razor Publishing, 2004), 238.

36. Frederick Douglass, "A Plea for Free Speech in Boston," speech delivered in Boston, Massachusetts, December 1860, in *Frederick Douglass: Selected Speeches and Writings*, ed. Philip S. Foner, abr. Yuval Taylor (Lawrence Hill Books, 2000), 314.

Chapter 8: Democratic Socialism: Marxism Lite

1. Karl Marx and Friedrich Engels, *The German Ideology,* in *Collected Works*, vol. 5 (International Publishers, 1976), 47.
2. Karl Marx, "Critique of the Gotha Programme," in *Karl Marx Friederich Engels Collected Works, vol. 24, Marx and Engels: 1874–1883*, trans. Richard Dixon et al. (Progress Publishers, 1989), 87.
3. Joseph A. Schumpeter, *Capitalism, Socialism and Democracy* (Harper & Brothers, 1942), 5–6.
4. See *Money, Greed and God* (HarperOne, 2010) by Jay Richards for more on this topic.
5. Karl Marx and Friedrich Engels, *The Communist Manifesto* (International Publishers, 2024), 22.
6. Marx and Engels, *The Communist Manifesto*, 30.
7. Joseph Stalin in a speech delivered at the First All-Union Congress of Collective Farm Shock Brigadiers, February 19, 1933. Source: *Works*, vol. 13, 1930–January 1934 (Foreign Languages Publishing House, Moscow, 1954), https://www.marxists.org/reference/archive/stalin/works/1933/02/19.htm.
8. Thomas Sowell, *The Vision of the Anointed: Self-Congratulation as a Basis for Social Policy* (Basic Books, 1995), 113.
9. Thomas Jefferson, "Letter to Thomas Cooper, November 29, 1802," in *The Writings of Thomas Jefferson,* ed. Paul Leicester Ford, vol. 8. (G. P. Putnam's Sons, 189), 181–82.
10. Benjamin Franklin, remarks recorded by James McHenry, September 18, 1787, in *Documents Illustrative of the Formation of the Union of the American States,* ed. Charles C. Tansill (Government Printing Office, 1927), 978–79.
11. Margaret Thatcher in a television interview with Llew Gardner, *This Week*, Thames Television, February 5, 1976. Quoted in *Margaret Thatcher, The Path to Power* (HarperCollins, 1995), 355.
12. Gerald L. K. Smith, quoted in Wikipedia, https://en.wikipedia.org/wiki/Gerald_L._K._Smith#cite_note-34.
13. Frank Camp, "INTERVIEW (Part I): Swedish Author Johan Norberg on the Devastating Impact of Socialism, and What It Could Cost the

US," *Daily Wire*, February 14, 2020, https://www.dailywire.com/news/interview-part-i-swedish-author-johan-norberg-on-the-devastating-impact-of-socialism-and-what-it-could-cost-the-u-s.

14. Marvin Olasky, "The View from 'Doralzuela,'" *World Magazine*, May 25, 2019, https://world.wng.org/2019/05/the_view_from_doralzuela.

15. John Stonestreet and Timothy D. Padgett, "Why Socialism Always Fails," November 25, 2025, Breakpoint, https://breakpoint.org/why-socialism-always-fails/.

16. Winston S. Churchill, speech to the House of Commons, October 22, 1945, in *Hansard's Parliamentary Debates*, 5th ser., vol. 414 (1945), col. 579.

17. Nazım Hikmet, "Kerem Gibi," in *Bütün Şiirleri (Complete Poems)* (Istanbul: YKY), various editions (first published 1955 or 1956 depending on the collection).

18. George Orwell, *Animal Farm: A Fairy Story* (Houghton Mifflin Harcourt, 2009), 192.

19. For the full context of this summary, please see Francis A. Schaeffer, *How Should We Then Live?: The Rise and Decline of Western Thought and Culture* (Crossway Books, 1976), chapter 13, esp. 225–26.

Chapter 9: What Did Marx Get Wrong and Moody Get Right?

1. Robert Owen, "Man's Character Is Formed for Him, Not by Him," in *A New View of Society*; or *Essays on the Formation of Character*, 3rd ed. (Cadell & Davies, 1817), 45–50.

2. Marx and Engels, *The Communist Manifesto* (International Publishers, 2024), 29–30.

Part Two: Dwight L. Moody

Introduction from Gregg Quiggle

1. He put it this way, "I've had more trouble with D. L. Moody than any other man who has crossed my path." D. L. Moody, *The Overcoming Life*, 16. https://archive.org/details/overcominglife0000dlmo/page/16/mode/2up.

2. R. A. Torrey, "Why God Used D. L. Moody," Wholesome Words, https://www.wholesomewords.org/biography/biomoody6.html.

3. A portion of this part of the book used by permission from my previous book for Moody Publishers titled, *Bread and Bibles: D. L. Moody's Evangelism and Social Action* (2024). It also includes portions from my dissertation, "An Analysis of Dwight Moody's Urban Social Vision," PhD thesis, The Open University, 2010. Portions of chapter 7 were previously published in *Standing Firm: The Doctrinal Commitments of Moody Bible Institute* (Moody, 2019). Several paragraphs are based on a previously published chapter titled, "D. L. Moody: First International Evangelist," in *A Legacy of Preaching*, eds. Benjamin K. Forest et al. (Zondervan, 2018) 241–56. There is also some material based on a chapter titled "Moody on Prayer," in *A Praying People: Essays Inspired by Dwight Moody*, eds. James Spencer and Ashish Varma (Wipf and Stock, 2013), 11–26.

Chapter 1: Introducing Mr. Moody

1. Lyle Dorsett, *A Passion for Souls: The Life of D. L. Moody* (Moody Publishers, 1997), 66–67.
2. The best survey of Moody and media is Bruce Evensen, *God's Man for the Gilded Age* (Oxford, 2003).
3. *New York Times*, December 24, 1899, 22. Quoted in Evensen, 9.
4. *Boston Journal*, December 27, 1899, 3. Quoted in Evensen, 9.
5. *Chicago Daily News*, December 22, 1899, 4. Quoted in Evensen, 8.
6. *Manchester Guardian*, December 23, 1899, 9. Quoted in Evensen, 10.
7. *Evening News* (London), December 23, 1899, 2. Quoted in Evensen, 10.
8. *The Catholic World*, quoted in John McDowell, *What D. L. Moody Means to Me: An Anthology of Appreciation and Appraisals of the Beloved Founder of the Northfield Schools* (The Northfield Schools, 1937), 13, 28.
9. *Boston Evening Transcript*, December 22, 1899, 6. Quoted in Evensen, 12. The full quote can be found J. Wilbur Chapman, *The Life and Work of D. L. Moody* (American Bible House, 1900), 424.
10. Thomas Kidd, "Why Dwight Moody Was Billy Graham's Key Predecessor," The Gospel Coalition, March 13, 2018, https://www.thegospelcoalition.org/blogs/evangelical-history/dwight-moody-billy-grahams-key-predecessor/.
11. William R. Moody, *Life of Moody by His Son* (Fleming H. Revell, 1900), frontispiece.

12. D. L. Moody Digital Archive, https://www.moodycenter.org/archives.

13. George Marsden, *Fundamentalism and American Culture* (Oxford University Press, 1980), 33.

14. Stanley Gundry, *Love Them In: The Life and Theology of Dwight Moody* (Baker Book House, 1976), 10. Gundry cites Will H. Houghton and Chas. T. Cook, *Tell Me About Moody* (Marshall, Morgan & Scott, 1936), 117. For similar statistical estimates, see Pollock, *Moody: A Biographical Portrait*, 166, 242, 283–84.

15. J. Wilbur Chapman, *The Life and Work of D. L. Moody* (American Bible House, 1900) vi, 17–21.

16. Ralph D. Winter, "Four Men, Three Eras, Two Transitions: Modern Missions," https://www.perspectivesonmission.com/resources/Session06_Winter_4Men3Eras2Transitions.pdf.

17. Ralph Winter, "The Student Volunteers of 1886, Their Heirs, and the Year 2000," *International Journal of Frontier Missions,* vol. 2, no. 2 April 1985, 156. Winter's article provides an excellent overview.

18. See for example Lyman Beecher, *A Plea for the West* (1835) and Josiah Strong, *Our Country: Its Possible Future and Its Present Crisis* (1885). Treatments of anti-Catholicism in America include: Mark S. Massa, SJ, *Anti-Catholicism in America: The Last Acceptable Prejudice* (Crossroad, 2003); Ray Allen Billington, *The Protestant Crusade, 1800–1860: A Study of the Origins of American Nativism* (Quadrangle Books, 1964); Katie Oxx, *The Nativist Movement in America: Religious Conflict in the 19th Century* (Routledge, 2013); Philip Jenkins, *The New Anti-Catholicism: The Last Acceptable Prejudice* (Oxford University Press, 2003).

19. John Pollock, *Moody: A Biographical Portrait of the Pacesetter in Modern Mass Evangelism* (Macmillan, 1963), 60.

20. D. L. Moody, *New Sermons, Addresses and Prayers by Dwight Lyman Moody* (Thompson & Wakefield, 1877), 14.

21. Ibid., 485.

22. W. H. Daniels, *Moody: His Words, Work, and Workers* (Nelson & Phillips, 1877), 431–32.

23. D. L. Moody, *Men of the Bible* (Bible Institute Colportage Association, 1898), 67

24. 1895 January, Record of Christian Work, Volume 14, Number 1, "Hints and Helps, Nuggets from Mr. Moody's Bible," Quote Page 13, Column 1, Fleming H. Revell Company, Chicago, Illinois.
25. W. H. Daniels, *D. L. Moody and His Work* (American Publishing, 1875), 116. Daniels notes that on one New Years Day alone, Moody visited 200 families.
26. Charles Hambrick-Stowe, *Charles G. Finney and the Spirit of American Evangelicalism* (1996), 174. Elsewhere in this work, Finney is described as "forever chary of any diversion, no matter how worthy in itself, from the work of saving souls," 111. See also, Jim Rice, "The Roots of Justice Revival," *Sojourners Magazine*, April 2008, https://sojo.net/magazine/april-2008/roots-justice-revival.
27. For a detailed study, see Alex Diprima, *Spurgeon and the Poor: How the Gospel Compels Christian Social Concern* (Reformation Heritage Books, 2023).
28. Daniels, *Moody: His Words, Work, and Workers*, 256.
29. David Bebbington, "How Moody Changed Revivalism," Christian History Institute, https://christianhistoryinstitute.org/magazine/article/how-moody-changed-revivalism#:~:text=Moody%20reinforced%20the%20existing%20link,the%20visit%20of%20the%20evangelists.
30. Dennis Olenik, *The Social Philosophy of D. L. Moody* (Northern Illinois University, 1964), 39
31. The biographies by Kevin Belmonte (*D. L. Moody, A Life: Innovator, Evangelist, World Changer*) and Lyle Dorsett (*A Passion for Souls: The Life of D. L. Moody*) are both excellent.

Chapter 2: Childhood, Poverty, and Conversion

1. M. Laird Simons, *Holding the Fort: Comprising Sermons and Addresses at the Great Revival Meetings Conducted by Moody and Sankey* (Quaker City Publishing, 1877), 198–99.
2. A similar incident from the life of Phillips Brooks supports this interpretation. In a letter dated November 22, 1927, a Rev. William Lawrence writes to William Moody in response to William's question about Phillips Brooks and baptism. He confirms Brooks was baptized as an infant by a Unitarian in the name of the Father, the Son, and the Holy Ghost. Brooks maintained, "In his judgment and knowledge his baptism was valid." Moody Bible Institute Archives.

3. W. H. Daniels, *Moody: His Words, Work, and Workers* (Nelson & Phillips, 1877), 12.
4. Lyle Dorsett, *A Passion for Souls: The Life of D. L. Moody* (Moody Publishers, 1997), 7.
5. William R. Moody, *Life of Moody by His Son* (Fleming H. Revell, 1900), 21.
6. Richard Ellsworth Day, *Bush Aglow: The Life Story of Dwight Lyman Moody, Commoner of Northfield* (The Judson Press, 1936), 40.
7. J. Wilbur Chapman, *The Life and Work of D. L. Moody* (American Bible House, 1900), 65.
8. Paul Dwight Moody and Arthur Percy Fitt, *The Shorter Life of D. L. Moody* (BICA, 1900), 14. See also William R. Moody, *Life of Moody*, 26.
9. Charles Goss, *Echoes from the Platform and Pulpit* (A. O. Worthington, 1900), 96.
10. Ibid., 96, 97.
11. Timothy George, ed., *Mr. Moody and the Evangelical Tradition* (T&T Clark, 2004), 4–5.
12. Goss, *Echoes from the Pulpit*, 97.
13. Rev. Tony Cooke, "Visit to D. L. Moody Museum," https://tonycooke.org/articles-by-tony-cooke/d-l-moodys-conversion-and-rough-start/.
14. D. L. Moody, letter to brother, March 17, 1857, Moody Bible Institute Archives, Chicago, IL.
15. Moody, *Life*, 41.
16. Moody, *Life*, 44.
17. Langdon S. Ward, deacon of the Mount Vernon Church, "Dwight L. Moody's experience 1855–56," typescript, Special Collections, Yale Divinity School Library, D. L. Moody Papers.
18. Moody, *Life*, 44–45.
19. Moody, *Life*, 41.
20. Quoted in George D. Johnson, *What Will a Man Give in Exchange for His Soul?* (Light of the Savior Ministries, 2011), 114.

Chapter 3: A Man in a Hurry

1. Quoted in Lyle Dorsett, "Dwight L. Moody: Evangelist and Master Disciple Maker," C. S. Lewis Institute, September 6, 2011, https://www.cslewisinstitute.org/resources/dwight-l-moody-evangelist-and-master-disciple-maker/#:~:text=An%20Impetuous%20Move,Chicago's%20lucrative%20real%20estate%20market.
2. Leslie Landrigan, "Dwight L. Moody, Yankee Preacher, Meets Abe Lincoln in Little Hell," https://newenglandhistoricalsociety.com/dwight-l-moody-yankee-preacher-meets-abe-lincoln-in-little-hell/.
3. W. H. Daniels, *D. L. Moody and His Work* (American Publishing, 1875), 37.
4. Northrop, H. Davenport, *Life and Labors of Dwight L. Moody, the Great Evangelist: Containing a Full Account of His Great Career, His Remarkable Trait of Character . . . Including His Brilliant Discourses, Pithy Sayings, Famous Conferences at Northfield, Glowing Tributes to His Life and Labors from the Pulpit, the Press, Etc., Etc.* (R.A.H., 1900), 468.
5. J. Wilbur Chapman, *The Life and Work of D. L. Moody* (American Bible House, 1900), 97, 98.
6. Daniels, *D. L Moody and His Work*, 44. See also John Pollock, *Moody: The Biography*, chapter 5, "The Children's Friend" (Baker Pub Group, 1997), for additional anecdotes of Moody's recruitment techniques.
7. August J. Fry, *D. L. Moody: The Formative Years, 1856–1873* (University of Chicago, 1955), 2.
8. Charles Goss, *Echoes from the Platform and Pulpit* (A. O. Worthington, 1900), 310.
9. Ibid., 312.
10. Landrigan, "Dwight L. Moody, Yankee Preacher, Meets Abe Lincoln in Little Hell."
11. Lyle Dorsett, *A Passion for Souls: The Life of D. L. Moody* (Moody Publishers, 1997), 76.
12. Moody, quoted in Goss, *Echoes from the Pulpit*, 479–82.
13. Quoted in Emmett Dedmon, *Great Enterprises: 100 Years of the YMCA of Metropolitan Chicago* (Rand McNally, 1957), 54–55.
14. D. L. Moody, letter to brother Samuel, January 13, 1862, Moody Bible Institute Archives, Chicago, IL.

15. Dedmon, *Great Enterprises: 100 Years of the YMCA of Metropolitan Chicago.* See especially chapters 3 and 4.

16. Dorsett, *Passion*, 77

17. Ibid., 78.

18. Daniels, *D. L. Moody and His Work*, 87.

19. Ibid.

20. Dorsett, *Passion*, 77–86. In this section Dorsett describes Moody's work with the YMCA.

21. *Centennial Brochure* (Moody Bible Institute, April 7, 2007). Elsewhere the purpose is described as seeking "the spiritual good of the soldiers . . . and incidentally their intellectual improvement and social and physical comfort." Lemuel Moss, *Annals of the United States Christian Commission* (J. B. Lippincott, 1868), 107.

22. William R. Moody, *Life of Moody by His Son* (Fleming H. Revell, 1900), 82–84.

23. Ibid., 85.

24. "The Battle of Shiloh," https://npshistory.com/publications/civil_war_series/22/sec16.htm#:~:text=Shiloh%2C%20or%20Pittsburg%20Landing%2C%20as%20it%20was,of%201812%2C%20and%20Mexican%20War)%20added%20together.

25. "The FReeper Foxhole Revisits the Battle of Shiloh – March 20th, 2004," https://freerepublic.com/focus/f-vetscor/1101822/posts?page=6.

26. Stanley Gundry, *Love Them In: The Life and Theology of D. L. Moody* (Baker Book House, 1976), 100. In another letter to his mother dated February 4, 1863, Moody writes of attending to the sick and wounded of Rosencrans' Army. Rosencrans' Union forces were defeated at the battles of Murfreesboro and Chickamauga in Tennessee and Georgia. D. L. Moody, letter to mother, February 4, 1863, Special Collections, Yale Divinity School Library, D. L. Moody Papers.

27. Chapman, *Life and Work*, 183; and Myron Chartier, *The Social Views of Dwight L. Moody and Their Relation to the Workingman of 1860–1900* (Fort Hays Kansas State College, 1969), 41.

28. Dorsett, *Passion*, 122–23.

29. Ibid.

30. Ibid., 122.

31. Dorsett, *Passion*, 128, 148; and Don Sweeting, "Turning Point," in George, 41–42.

32. William in his biography notes, "Mrs. Moody was at that time also suffering from asthma, and their physician had suggested that a sea voyage, with an entire change of air and scene was desirable." William R. Moody, *Life of Moody*, 131.

Chapter 4: Learning from His Brethren in the United Kingdom

1. D. L. Moody, letter to mother, London, England, March 19, 1867, Biographical Files, Moody Bible Institute Archives, Chicago, IL.
2. Lyle Dorsett, *A Passion for Souls: The Life of D. L. Moody* (Moody Publishers, 1997), 86.
3. John Pollock, *Moody Without Sankey* (Hodder & Stoughton, 1963), 66.
4. Dorsett, *Passion*, 132, 133, 291, 396. Dorsett gives an extended account of this event and speaks of Spurgeon's influence on him.
5. Charles H. Spurgeon, Susannah Spurgeon, W. J. Harrald, *The Autobiography of Charles H. Spurgeon* (Curts & Jennings, 1900), 4:247.
6. Ibid., 247.
7. Dorsett, *Passion*, 396.
8. William R. Moody, *Life of Moody by His Son* (Fleming H. Revell, 1900), 447.
9. Ibid.
10. Staff writer, "How Spurgeon's Favorite Color Can Heal a Broken Nation," The Spurgeon Center, https://www.spurgeon.org/resource-library/blog-entries/how-spurgeons-favorite-color-can-heal-a-broken-nation/.
11. Alex DiPrima, "What Did Charles Spurgeon Think About Social Activism?," Center for Faith and Culture, June 18, 2020, https://cfc.sebts.edu/faith-and-politics/what-did-charles-spurgeon-think-about-social-activism/#:~:text=His%20commentary%20on%20political%20issues, Democratic%20party%20in%20America%20today.
12. Ibid.

13. Ibid.

14. Ibid.

15. *New York Times*, March 12, 1890, 9.

16. John Pollock, *Moody Without Sankey* (Hodder & Stoughton, 1963), 82; and Don Sweeting, "The Great Turning Point in the Life of D. L. Moody," in Timothy George, ed. *Mr. Moody and the Evangelical Tradition* (T&T Clark, 2004), 39–48. Although others have pointed out the role the Chicago fire played in Moody's life, I am particularly indebted to Sweeting's interpretation of this event.

17. Moody, *Life*, 147–48.

18. D. L. Moody (letter, November 24, 1871). A copy of this letter is in the *Moodyana* collection.

19. Moody, *Life*, 149.

20. Sweeting, in George, *Mr. Moody*, 39–48.

21. Mark Fackler, Christian History Institute, "The World Has Yet to See . . ."

    https://christianhistoryinstitute.org/magazine/article/world-has-yet-to-see.

22. R. A. Torrey, *Why God Used D. L. Moody* (Fleming H. Revell, 1923), 9–10.

23. Dorsett, *Passion*, 174–76.

24. Moody, *Life*, 152–69.

25. See "Christian History Timeline: Dwight L. Moody and His World," Christian History Institute, https://christianhistoryinstitute.org/magazine/article/moody-timeline. The two and one-half million figure is a total number of attendees and does not allow for people who attended more than once. See also, Dorsett, *Passion*, 206–207; and James F. Findlay Jr., *Dwight L. Moody: American Evangelist* (1837–1899) (1969; repr., Wipf & Stock, 2007), 171.

26. Moody, *Life*, 297–310. Again, this figure is total attendees and does not allow for people who attended more than once.

27. David Bebbington, *The Dominance of Evangelicalism: The Age of Spurgeon and Moody* (InterVarsity Press, 2005), 48; and Andrew Aird, *Glimpses of Old Glasgow* (Aird & Coghill, 1894), 200.

28. David Bebbington, "Moody as a Transatlantic Evangelical," in Timothy George, ed., *Mr. Moody and the Evangelical Tradition* (T&T Clark, 2004), 87.

29. Myron Chartier, *The Social Views of Dwight L. Moody and Their Relation to the Workingman of 1860–1900* (Hays Kansas State College, 1969), 58.

30. William Reid, *Authentic Records of Revival Now in Progress in the United Kingdom* (James Nisbet, 1860), 452.

31. Carubbers Christian Centre, "History," https://www.carrubbers.org/about/us.php#history.

32. Chartier, *Social Views*, 59.

33. Chartier, 59, 60.

Chapter 5: Education, Practical and Biblical

1. The quote is by President H. G. Weston, of the *Crozer Theological Seminary*, as quoted in William R. Moody, *Life of Moody by His Son* (Fleming H. Revell, 1900), 563.

2. Henry Rankin, *Handbook of the Northfield Seminary and the Mt. Hermon School* (Fleming H. Revell, 1889), 19.

3. Rankin, *Handbook of the Northfield Seminary*, 9–10.

4. Moody, *Life of Moody*, 337.

5. Lyle Dorsett, *A Passion for Souls: The Life of D. L. Moody* (Moody Publishers, 1997), 287–88. Dorsett points out that these early classes included Asians as well. He notes Booker T. Washington was invited to speak at the school and some of the early graduates returned to the American south to form orphanages for black children.

6. Rankin, *Handbook of the Northfield Seminary*, 24.

7. Burnham Carter, *So Much to Learn: The History of the Northfield Mount Hermon School in Commemoration of the One Hundredth Anniversary 1980* (Northfield Mount Hermon School, 1976), 49.

8. Ibid.

9. Timothy Gloege, *Guaranteed Pure: The Moody Bible Institute, Business, and the Making of Modern Evangelicalism* (University of North Carolina Press, 2015), 46–47. Gloege in pages 46–66 provides his read of the founding of the Institute. For my interpretation, see *Bread and Bibles*, Moody, 2024.

10. For a brief discussion see Erica Gunderson, "Ask Geoffrey: How Did Chicago Manage Epidemics Throughout Its History?," https://news.wttw.com/2020/04/09/ask-geoffrey-how-did-chicago-manage-epidemics-throughout-its-history.

11. James Findlay, "Moody, 'Gapmen,' and the Gospel: The Early Days of Moody Bible Institute," *Church History* 31, no. 3 (1962): 322–35. https://doi.org/10.2307/3163323. Quote from page 324. The quote raises the question of the effect of the Civil War on Moody. Given the link between Socialism and revolution, one wonders how the specter of another bloodbath like the Civil War factored into Moody's anxiety over labor unrest.

12. D. L. Moody, letter sent out by the Chicago Evangelistic Society, June 1887.

13. Gloege, *Guaranteed Pure*, 58.

14. "Guide to the World's Columbian Exposition of 1893 Collection 1892-1930," University of Chicago Library, 2023, https://www.lib.uchicago.edu/e/scrc/findingaids/view.php?eadid=ICU.SPCL.EXPO1893.

15. Moody, *Life*, 340.

16. Henry Burns Hartzler, Henry Burns, *Moody in Chicago: Or, The World's Fair Gospel Campaign: An Account of Six Months' Evangelistic Work in the City of Chicago and Vicinity During the Time of the World's Columbian Exposition, Conducted by Dwight L. Moody and His Associates* (Fleming H. Revell Co., 1894), 242.

17. "About Moody Publishers," https://www.moodypublishers.com/about-us.

18. G. W. Coleman, letter to D. L. Moody, January 24, 1899, Moody Bible Institute Archives, Chicago, IL. This letter contains details of the association's work in this regard. It includes a report on the current inventory of books and Bibles, the numbers of volumes sent to various prisons and plans to seek donations to increase the number of books available to be sent out. It also notes plans to translate books into Spanish for distribution. The letter ends with an account of the impact on the prisoners in one prison.

19. Moody, *Life*, 556–90. William Moody's biography gives extensive coverage to the funeral and memorials.

Chapter 6: Understanding the Cities of the 1800s

1. Josiah Strong, *Our Country: Its Possible Future and Its Present Crisis* (Baker & Tylor Co. for the American Home Missionary Society, 1885), 128, 129. Specifically, he writes, "Our fifty principal cities contain 39.3 per cent of our entire German population, and 45.8 per cent of the Irish. Our ten larger cities only nine per cent of the entire population, but 23 per cent of the foreign." He claimed, "While a little less than one-third of the population of the United States is foreign by birth or parentage, sixty-two per cent of the population of Cincinnati are foreign . . . sixty-three per cent of Boston, eighty-eight per cent of New York."

2. Strong, *Our Country*, 129–30.

3. On Roman Catholicism he opines, "Our fundamental ideas of society, therefore, are as radically opposed to Vaticanism as to imperialism, and it is as inconsistent with our liberties for Americans to yield allegiance to the Pope as to the Czar." Strong, *Our Country*, 54. On alcohol he writes, "The saloon, together with the intemperance and the liquor power which it represents, is multiplied in the city." Ibid., 129. "Socialism," Strong claims, "not only centers in the city, but is almost confined to it; and the materials of its growth are multiplied with the growth of the city." Ibid., 132.

4. Strong, *Our Country*, 132–33.

5. Strong, *Our Country*, 143–44. Strong is also concerned about the rise of Roman Catholicism, alcoholism, and Socialism in the cities.

6. Sydney E. Ahlstrom, *A Religious History of the American People* (Yale University Press, 1974), 735. Between 1860 and 1900, the period during which Moody worked, 14 million immigrants arrived.

7. Chester Gillis, *Roman Catholicism in America* (Columbia University Press, 1999), 60–61. In 1820, Roman Catholics comprised less than 1 percent of the population; by 1830, 3.8 percent; by 1840, 5.8 percent; and by 1850, 12.5 percent.

8. Howard P. Chudacoff and Judith E. Smith, *The Evolution of American Urban Society*, 5th ed. (Prentice Hall, 2000), 122. The percentages were determined by taking the number of city inhabitants and dividing them by the total population of the United States. The population figures were taken from the United States census figures of 1860 and 1910, respectively. The numbers from 1860 include the slave population.

9. For a brief article on the situation see this from the Newberry Library in Chicago, https://dcc.newberry.org/?p=14434. See also this short essay from North Illinois University library https://digital.lib.niu.edu/illinois/gildedage/labor.

10. Ibid.

11. Anne Bramley, "How Chicago's Slaughterhouse Spectacles Paved the Way for Big Meat," NPR, December 3, 2015, https://www.npr.org/sections/thesalt/2015/12/03/458314767/how-chicago-s-slaughter-house-spectacles-paved-the-way-for-big-meat. For a complete look at the history of the Stockyards see, Dominic A. Pacyga's *Slaughterhouse: Chicago's Union Stock Yard and the World It Made* (University of Chicago Press, 2015).

12. Frederick Law Olmsted, *A Journey Through Texas: Or, A Saddle-Trip on the Southwestern Frontier: With a Statistical Appendix* (Dix, Edwards & Co., 1857), 9.

13. "The Union Stockyards: 'A Story of American Capitalism,'" https://www.wttw.com/chicago-stories/union-stockyards/the-union-stock-yards-a-story-of-american-capitalism.

14. Daniel Miller, *City of the Century: The Epic of Chicago and the Making of America* (Simon and Schuster, 1996), 204–205. Miller noted Henry Ford modeled his assembly line on the packers' plants in Chicago.

15. Miller, *City of the Century*, 123, 427.

16. Ibid.

17. The founder of the Women's Christian Temperance Union was Frances Willard. She was an early associate of Moody who worked with him on his 1877 campaign in Boston. For more details, see Lyle Dorsett, *A Passion for Souls: The Life of D. L. Moody* (Moody Publishers, 1997), 252–54.

18. Quoted in William R. Moody, *Life of Moody by His Son* (Fleming H. Revell, 1900), 263. His close associate, Henry Drummond, echoed Moody's call in an 1893 work titled *The City Without a Church*. In the work, Drummond argues that world redemption is dependent on urban Christianization.

19. This is demonstrated by the *1851 Census of the Population of England and Wales*. The census revealed that for the first time in the history of any significant nation, more people lived in towns than in rural areas. In

fact, it has been estimated that from 1841 to 1901, the rural areas of England and Wales lost more than 4 million people due to internal migration. Of these, 3 million headed for the towns, at a rate of more than half a million per decade. Furthermore, by 1881, 50 percent of Britain's populace lived in cities of 20,000 or more. By 1891, fully 72 percent of the population of England and Wales was categorized as urban. From 1801 to 1911, the urban population increased nearly by a factor of ten, from 3.5 to 32 million, leading Bédarida to describe this phenomena as "galloping urbanization." F. A Bédarida, *Social History of England, 1851–1975,* trans. A. S. Forster (Methuen, 1979), 32.

20. Susan Isaac, "Holme's Great Metropolis: or, Views of London in the Nineteenth Century (and Now)," Royal College of Surgeons of England, January 19, 2018, https://www.rcseng.ac.uk/library-and-publications/library/blog/holmes-great-metropolis/.

21. Porter, *London*, 364.

22. For a look at Belfast, see Estyn Evans and Emrys Jones, "The Growth of Belfast," in *The Town Planning Review*, 26, no. 2 (July 1955), 92–111. For accounts of the industrial revolution in Scotland, see R. H. Campbell, *Scotland Since 1707: The Rise of an Industrial Society* (John Donald Publishers, 1965), and *The Rise and Fall of Scottish Industry 1707–1939* (John Donald Publishers, 1980); Anthony Slaven, *The Development of the West of Scotland 1750–1960,* (Routledge & K. Paul, 1975); S. G. E. Lythe and J. Butt, *An Economic History of Scotland, 1100–1939* (Blackie, 1975); B. Lenman, *An Economic History of Modern Scotland 1660–1976* (B. T. Batsford Ltd., 1977); and C. H. Lee, "Modern Economic Growth and Structural Change in Scotland: the Service Sector Reconsidered," *Scottish Economic and Social History* 3, no. 3 (1983), 115–35, which provides a critique of these and other approaches to Scottish economic growth.

23. Sean Damer, *Glasgow: Going for a Song* (Lawrence & Wishart, 1990), 71–103, 107–136.

24. Billy Graham, "The Evangelist and His Preaching: We Set Forth the Truth Plainly," in *The Work of an Evangelist* (World Wide Publications, 1984), https://www.preaching.com/sermons/ministry-we-set-forth-the-truth-plainly/.

25. "Acceptance Address by the Rev. Dr. Billy Graham," May 18, 1982, https://www.templetonprize.org/laureate-sub/address-by-the-reverend-dr-billy-graham/.

26. "Letters to A. P. Fitt," *Moodyana Collection*, Moody Bible Institute Archives, Chicago, IL.

27. For a more detailed discussion, see Myron Chartier, *The Social Views of Dwight L. Moody* and *Their Relation to the Workingman of 1860–1900* (Hays Kansas State College, 1969), *17–34.*

28. D. L. Moody, *Bible Characters* (Revell, 1888), 105.

29. Chartier, *The Social Views of D. L. Moody*, 18.

30. Ibid., 18, 19.

31. *Stanley Gundry, Love Them In: The Life and Theology of D. L. Moody* (Baker Book House, 1976), 151.

32. Quoted in Chartier, 25.

33. Gundry, *Love Them In*, 151. Gundry cites numerous of Moody's published sermons in support.

34. David Bebbington, *The Dominance of Evangelicalism: The Age of Spurgeon and Moody* (InterVarsity Press, 2005), 48, 49.

35. James F. Findlay Jr., *Dwight L. Moody: American Evangelist* (1837–1899) (1969; repr., Wipf & Stock, 2007), 279.

36. Specifically, if Moody were "endeavoring to change the relation of the black and white races," he would face the "contempt and abhorrence of our entire people." *Liberal Christian*, 30 (May 20, 1876), 9; letter to the *Atlanta Constitution* (no date), quoted in the *New York Times*, May 10, 1876.

37. Whittle Diary, April 28, 1876. Whittle claimed that "not to have done it would have . . . kept the white people away" and that there was "no way we could carry on the meetings" without them being segregated. One of the reasons Whittle knew the South was he had served on General Sherman's staff during his march to the sea during the Civil War. Dorsett indicates the diary was lost from the archives of Moody Bible Institute.

38. This analysis is based on more than seventy-five contemporary news accounts for Chattanooga (Jan. 25–31), Knoxville (Jan. 28–31), Nashville (Feb. 2–4), and Memphis, Tennessee (Feb. 5–8); New Orleans, Louisiana (Feb. 9–19); Galveston (Feb. 21–28), San Antonio (Feb. 28–March 2), and Dallas, Texas (March 4–7); Mobile (March 10–13) and Selma, Alabama (March 14–18); Charleston (March

23–28) and Columbia, South Carolina (March 31–April 1); Atlanta, Georgia (April 2–12) and Norfolk, Virginia (April 13–21). See also local news accounts for Louisville, Kentucky (Jan. 1–Feb. 12, 1888), and Richmond, Virginia (March 26–April 12, 1894). For an account of the Texas meetings, see Blum, Edward J. Blum, *Reforging the White Republic: Race, Religion, and American Nationalism, 1865–1898* (Louisiana State University, 2005), 144.

39. For Grimke, see Francis J. Grimké, "Mr. Moody and the Color Question in the South," *The Independent*, July 22, 1886, 7. And *Works of Francis Grimké*, vol. 3, Carter G. Woodson, ed. (The Associated Publishers, 1942), 420. For Wells see, Alfreda M. Duster, ed., *Crusade for Justice: The Autobiography of Ida B. Wells* (University of Chicago Press, 1970), 111–12, 151. And Miriam Decosta-Willis, ed., *The Memphis Diary of Ida B. Wells, An Intimate Portrait of the Activist as a Young Woman* (Beacon Press, 1995), 41–42.

40. Timothy Gloege, *Guaranteed Pure: The Moody Bible Institute, Business, and the Making of Modern Evangelicalism* (Function). Kindle edition, 51–52.

41. For my interpretation, see Gregg Quiggle, *Bread and Bibles* (Moody, 2024), 185–99. See also; Edward J. Blum, *Reforging the White Republic: Race, Religion, and American Nationalism, 1865–1898* (Louisiana State University, 2005). Blum argued that Moody's message was instrumental in rebuilding the white republic by sanctifying reconciliation among northern and southern whites at the expense of African Americans. Specifically, Blum charged Moody with keeping quiet in the face of racial prejudice, choosing unity among whites over human unity.

42. D. L. Moody, *The Overcoming Life*, 16. https://archive.org/details/overcominglife0000dlmo/page/16/mode/2up.

Chapter 7: Sin, the Gospel, and the Human Predicament

1. The best survey of Moody's theology remains Stanley Gundry, *Love Them In: The Life and Theology of Dwight Moody* (Baker Book House, 1976).

2. In his book *Love Them In*, Gundry traces these three themes throughout most of Moody's sermons. See also George M. Marsden's book, *Fundamentalism and American Culture*, 35. In addition, one of Moody's personal Bibles at the archives in Northfield Schools contains the following comment on the inner leaf: "This book teaches three things, Ruin, Redemption, Regeneration."

3. W. H. Daniels, *Moody: His Words, Work, and Workers* (Nelson & Phillips, 1877), 256.
4. Dwight Moody, *New Sermons, Addresses and Prayers by Dwight Lyman Moody* (Thompson & Wakefield, 1877), 128.
5. D. L. Moody, *Twelve Select Sermons* (Fleming F. Revel, 1881), 21.
6. Ibid., 21.
7. Daniels, *Moody: His Words, Work, and Workers,* 414–21.
8. D. L. Moody, *Moody's Sermons, Addresses and Prayers* (N. D. Thompson, 1877), 259.
9. D. L. Moody, *Wondrous Love: Fifteen Addresses* (J. E. Hawkins, 1875). 127.
10. Quoted by Gundry in *Love Them In*, 112.
11. Ibid., 111.
12. Ibid., 112.
13. Ibid., 172.
14. D. L. Moody, *Heaven* (1880; repr., Moody Press, 1995), 104.
15. D. L. Moody, *Twelve Select Sermons*, 35.
16. Sermon delivered by Dwight L. Moody in the Free Church Assembly Hall, Edinburgh, Scotland, December, 9, 1873, http://biblebaptist-churchnaples.org/pages/Library/Moody/blood.html.
17. D. L. Moody, *Twelve Select Sermons*, 120.
18. D. L. Moody, *Ten Select Sermons* (Chicago, 1881), 26.
19. Ibid., 28.
20. Quoted by Gundry in *Love Them In*, 102.
21. D. L. Moody, "*To All People," Comprising Sermons, Bible Readings, Temperance Addresses, and Prayer Meeting Talks, Delivered in the Boston Tabernacle by Dwight Moody* (E. B. Treat, 1877), 199.
22. D. L. Moody, *The Way to God and How to Find It* (Fleming H. Revell, 1884), 23.
23. Ibid., 25–26.
24. Ibid., 27.

25. Ibid., 30.

26. Quoted in Gundry, *Love Them In*, 130.

27. John McDowell, *What D. L. Moody Means to Me: An Anthology of Appreciation and Appraisals of the Beloved Founder of the Northfield Schools* (The Northfield Schools, 1937), 17.

28. D. L. Moody, *Secret Power: Or the Secret of Success in Christian Life and Work* (Fleming H. Revell, 1881), 10.

29. Ibid., 50.

30. Major Billy Francis, "Dwight L. Moody: Consider the Life of Dwight L. Moody and Then Allow the Needle of Your Heart to Point to Jesus!," *Peer Magazine*, April 2022, https://peermag.org/articles/dwight-l-moody/.

31. William R. Moody, *Life of Moody by His Son* (Fleming H. Revell, 1900), 437, 438.

32. D. L. Moody, *Anecdotes and illustrations of D.L. Moody: related by him in his revival work* (Rhodes and McClure, 1877), 46.

33. L. T. Remlap, ed., *The Gospel Awakening: Comprising the Sermons and Addresses, Prayer Meeting Talks and Bible Readings, of the Great Revival Meetings, Conducted by Moody and Sankey, in the Cities of Philadelphia, New York, Chicago and Boston, with the Proceedings of the Christian Conventions of Ministers and Laymen. From Verbatim Reports . . . Also the Lives of D. L. Moody, I. D. Sankey, P. P. Bliss, Rev. Joseph Cook, D. W. Whittle, Rev. G. F. Pentecost and Frances E. Willard* (Fairbanks and Palmer Publishing Co., 1885), 51–52.

34. Ibid., 52.

35. D. L. Moody, *"To All People," Comprising Sermons, Bible readings, Temperance Addresses, and Prayer Meeting Talks, delivered in the Boston Tabernacle by Dwight Moody.* (E. B. Treat, 1877), 136, 137.

36. D. L. Moody, *The Overcoming Life*, 17, 18, https://archive.org/details/overcominglife0000dlmo/page/16/mode/2up.

37. There are actually two collections of Moody's talks on temperance. The one referenced above is James B. Dunn, ed., *Moody's Talks on Temperance: With anecdotes and incidents in connection with the Tabernacle temperance work in Boston* (National Temperance Society and Publication House, 1877); and Daniels, *Moody: His Words, Work, and Workers.*

38. D. L. Moody, *To All People*, 450–51.
39. Quoted in James F. Findlay Jr., *Dwight L. Moody: American Evangelist (1837–1899)* (1969; repr., Wipf & Stock, 2007), 274–75.
40. Henry Rankin, *Handbook of the Northfield Seminary and the Mt. Hermon School* (Fleming F. Revel, 1899). This is noted throughout.
41. D. L. Moody, *To All People*, 487.
42. In one sermon, Moody tells of a man who refused to work, claiming he was studying the philosophy of pauperism. The man came seeking help for his family. Moody cared for the family and gave nothing to the man. He advised, "It is not charity to help them. If a man will not work, let him starve." For a full account, see Dwight Moody, *The New Sermons of Dwight Moody* (J. W. Goodspeed, 1880), 604, 605.
43. August J. Fry, *D. L. Moody: The Formative Years, 1856–1873* (University of Chicago Press, 1955), 42.
44. Dorsett, *Passion*, 379, 380.
45. Quoted in Daniels, *Moody: His Words, Work, and Workers*, 332.
46. Quoted in Gundry, *Love Them In*, 151.
47. *New York Times*, March 12, 1890, 9.

Chapter 8: A Life Well Lived

1. D. L. Moody, "*To the Work! To the Work!*": *Exhortations to Christians* (Moody Press, 1884), 131–32.
2. John McDowell, *What D. L. Moody Means to Me: An Anthology of Appreciations and Appraisals of the Beloved founder of the Northfield Schools* (The Northfield Schools, 1937), 8.
3. William R. Moody, *Life of Moody by His Son* (Fleming H. Revell, 1900), 248.
4. W. H. Daniels, *Moody: His Words, Work, and Workers* (Nelson & Phillips, 1877), 254.
5. R. A. Torrey, *Why God Used D. L. Moody* (Fleming H. Revell, 1923), 29, https://archive.org/details/whygoduseddlmood00torr_1/page/28/mode/2up.
6. Ibid., 33–36. Italics original.

7. For example, see Timothy Gloege, *Guaranteed Pure: The Moody Bible Institute, Business, and the Making of Modern Evangelicalism*, 48–65.

8. David Bebbington, *The Dominance of Evangelicalism: The Age of Spurgeon and Moody* (InterVarsity Press, 2005), 48.

9. David Bebbington, in "How Moody Changed Revivalism," Christian History Institute, https://christianhistoryinstitute.org/magazine/article/how-moody-changed-revivalism.

10. Probably the best book on the Social Gospel is Walter Rauschenbusch's *A Theology for the Social Gospel* (Macmillan, 1917).

11. Findlay notes and documents the continued esteem Gladden held for Moody late in their lives. James F. Findlay Jr., *Dwight L. Moody: American Evangelist* (1837–1899) (1969; repr., Wipf & Stock, 2007), 411.

12. See for example, Jacob Dorn, *Washington Gladden: Prophet of the Social Gospel* (Ohio State University Press, 1967). Dorn also described Gladden's high regard for Moody on page 380.

13. Eric Ames, "(A&SCRC) Similar Hymnals, Different Theologies," November 3, 2025, https://blogs.baylor.edu/baylorlibraries/2025/11/03/ascrc-similar-hymnals-different-theologies/.

14. Paul M. Minus, *Walter Rauschenbusch: American Reformer* (Oxford University Press, 1988), 56, 57.

15. Bebbington, *The Dominance*, 99, 100. Bebbington notes Shaftesbury's motives were mixed. He endorsed social rank, inequality, and deference. But he was also driven by his faith, specifically Matthew 25 where Christ asked in effect, "Have you labored for the physical and spiritual welfare of your fellow sinners?" As Shaftesbury put it, "to him that knoweth to do good and doeth it not, to him it is sin."

16. Bebbington, *The Dominance*, 100.

17. Blum acknowledges Moody's change but argues it was he should have spoken sooner. "It was a marvelous turn of events. The most noteworthy evangelical of the late nineteenth century took a clear stand against racial segregation. Tragically, it was too late. Moody no longer wielded the public power he once had, and this action garnered almost no attention from the press." Edward J. Blum, *Reforging the White Republic: Race, Religion, and American Nationalism, 1865–1898* (Louisiana State University, 2005), 144. For my interpretation, see Gregg Quiggle, *Bread and Bibles* (Moody, 2024), 185–199.

Two Tombstones, One Choice

1. "Tomb of Karl Marx," https://en.wikipedia.org/wiki/Tomb_of_Karl_Marx.
2. "Find Us Faithful," Jon Mohr (words and music), performed by Steve Green, 1988. Excerpt used by permission from the songwriters.

More by Dr. Lutzer

Running to Win | 365 Days of Timeless Wisdom and Biblical Insight for Growing Christians

Running to Win unites the timeless wisdom of the great evangelist D. L. Moody with the insightful scriptural reflections of longtime pastor Erwin Lutzer. Experience a year of devotions designed to draw you closer to Christ and guide you toward lasting purpose.

Why Doesn't God Answer My Prayers? | A Biblical Guide to God's Hidden Purposes

Dr. Lutzer helps us see God's love and guidance even when He seems silent. This biblical guide thoughtfully considers:

- When the person you love isn't healed.
- When the worst happens.
- When evil feels like it's winning.
- When promises are unfulfilled

  . . . and more.

When a Nation Forgets God | 7 Lessons We Must Learn from Nazi Germany

According to Dr. Lutzer, the German people's progression from civility to barbarity was not extraordinary, yet the Nazi regime will forever serve as an example of brutality and extreme racism run amok. We must take note of these lessons from history and be vigilant in our stand for truth, justice, and righteousness.

ALSO AVAILABLE AS EBOOKS | MOODYPUBLISHERS.COM

More by Dr. Lutzer

The Church in Babylon | Heeding the Call to Be a Light in the Darkness

Dr. Lutzer will walk you through the many parallels between the church in America and God's people in Babylon. Then he'll explain what we can learn from the Israelites about maintaining our faith in the midst of a pagan culture.

7 Reasons Why You Can Trust the Bible

With the current cultural onslaught against the authority of God's Word, *7 Reasons Why You Can Trust the Bible* is as timely as ever. Revised and expanded, it is an indispensable resource for lay Christians who want to know why they believe what they believe.

Who Are You to Judge? | Learning to Distinguish Between Truths, Half-Truths, and Lies

We live in a world that tolerates everything but judgment. What we don't realize is that right judgment is the key to right living. *Who Are You To Judge?* is Lutzer's word to a culture that hates being told how to live and to a church called to purity.